Giving Out Yards

Also by Tara Flynn

You're Grand:
The Irishwoman's Secret Guide to Life

GIVING OUT YARDS

The Art of Complaint, Irish Style

TARA FLYNN

HACHETTE
BOOKS
IRELAND

First published in Ireland in 2015 by
HACHETTE BOOKS IRELAND

A CIP catalogue record for this book is available from the British Library.

ISBN: 978 14736 2255 5

Typeset in Palatino by redrattledesign.com

Printed and bound in Great Britain by Clays Ltd, St Ives plc

Hachette Books Ireland policy is to use papers that are natural, renewable and recyclable products and made from wood grown in sustainable forests. The logging and manufacturing processes are expected to conform to the environmental regulations of the country of origin.

Hachette Books Ireland
8 Castlecourt Centre
Castleknock
Dublin 15, Ireland

A division of Hachette UK Ltd.
Carmelite House
50 Victoria Embankment
London EC4Y 0DZ

www.hachette.ie

★

For Noel Flynn, 1933–2015. My Dad.
Who taught me everything I'd ever need to know
about giving out.

★

Contents

Introduction

Giving Out: A Definition

The English language has a lot of words for 'complaint' or 'complaining' and, here in Ireland, we need every one of them. Grumbling, groaning, grouching, whining, bitching, griping, lamenting, bewailing – in fact, if we haven't bewailed something before breakfast, we don't feel properly set up for the day. Nobody complains like the Irish do. With terrible weather and centuries of oppression and the like, we have plenty to complain about. But even when we don't, we do. It's the national pastime. A way of bonding. Therapy.

As such, it's no exaggeration to say it's what we do best. We've raised it to an art form.

As we have such a special relationship with complaint,

there's no point calling it what everyone else does. In Ireland, we *give out*. If we're really riled up, we *give out yards*.

Why 'yards'? Yards, as we know, are an imperial measurement of length or something students use to drink ale from in beer-guzzling competitions. It seems 'feet' or 'pints' weren't enough to contain our moaning. Something like 'miles', however, might have been perceived as showing off. You can't be seen to think you're great, even at complaining. No one seems to agree on the origin (what a surprise), but it does seem that the art of complaint is too ancient to be measured in metres. So yards are what we give out in.

Whether you realise it or not, you probably gave out when you picked up this book:

It might have been the price. Books are expensive.

It might have been the cover design. Well, we love it.

It might have been the weight of it.

Maybe you're drawn to it, but when would you get the time to read? Who has that kind of luxury? Children? The Pope? Someone who has someone else to do everything for them, that's for sure.

Feel better now? Of course you do. Nothing tastes as good as giving out feels.

★

When We Say 'Irish Style', Who Are the Irish?

Part of giving out Irish style is that we sometimes even give out about who's 'Irish' in the first place. Well, it really depends on how far back you go. We didn't spring up on the island like mushrooms. We're firbolgs, Normans, Viking, Gaels, Angles, Saxons, pirates, saints and scholars, and loads of people from new places, too. It's nice not to be pinned down.

Irish people now come in all colours, shapes, sizes, beliefs, sexual orientations and – at long last – we're hearing transgender voices. There's plenty of room for all of us, since the Famine and constant emigration left us with tons of giving-out topics and a lot of space. We might as well fill it up. This way, loads of us can give out about how much fuller the country's getting, even though it's still half empty.

The term 'person living in Ireland' may be more technically correct but it does make it sound like someone's only here for a visit, when we hope they might actually like to stay. Then, we can all give out about each other.

It's not being born here that endows you with Give Out-ability. Even if you're only passing through, don't worry: everyone can give out and by the end of this book, you'll be giving out like a pro.

The Shushening

Many would agree that it's The Shushening that has us this keen on giving out.

The Shushening is our word for this book: 'oppression' is too much of a downer. And in Ireland, we hear oppression a lot. Nothing funny there.

So much of Irish history has involved us being squished and shushed out of being who we really are. Told what language to speak, told we were thick and only good for the odd postcard shoot, told to pay for other people's messes, told we weren't sexy, told what religion was the holiest – you get the picture. Shhh!

Even after we'd got rid of occupiers and snakes and power-mad holy fellas, and everyone got along just great, there still stretched a long shadow of grim. It definitely held us back but it was great for giving out about. We'd probably have colonised the moon by now if it hadn't been for The Shushening. We've been oppressed for so long, we'd almost miss it, so we subconsciously look for new ways to get squished and shushed and then give out about those.

The Shushening grew particularly shushy when the comedy double act of de Valera (Dev) and Archbishop John Charles McQuaid (ABJCMcQ) got together. They really tapped into our collective need for squishing and shushing and we're only just shaking off their hilarious influence today. Dev basically wanted lots of praying and Irish-speaking and women dancing at crossroads, like in olden times that never existed; McQuaid wanted lots of praying and for women to go away. Plus misery. Lots and lots of basically misery. They used fear to keep us good and squished, and it worked. But they died ages ago.

Or did they? Sometimes it can feel like they're still watching. Controlling things from wherever they ended up (which is debatable). Like a kind of haunting Statler and Waldorf, they seem to be still able to heckle, to disrupt the show, every time we get close to un-Shushening. And even if they really are gone, they certainly left plenty of Shushening agents. Their shadows still stretch across us sometimes. Luckily we even have torches on our phones now.

There are two utterly opposing sides to us. We have a beautiful ancient fighting spirit, but we've been squished for so long, sometimes it bursts out with inappropriate passion over something small. The big stuff is just too big sometimes. So we've found a middle ground, somewhere between expression and inaction. And that middle ground is giving out.

Where to Give Out

To do giving out right – i.e. like a historically squished Irish person – *It must not lead to doing anything.* No. Giving out yards is almost never followed by taking action.

It may be because the reason for complaint is so small that there's no real need, or conversely that it's so big it's pointless even trying to tackle it.

Regardless, as a nation, we are compelled to *talk about it*. And talk and talk and talk.

With so many different ways to give out now, why wouldn't we? Letters to newspapers, self-important blog posts, tweets, megaphones on the street, in the local with your mates or, best of all, on air if at all possible – don't worry, there's a method of giving out out there that suits you perfectly.

In fact, one wonders what we did before the wireless was invented. There must have been a lot of pressure on confession. We must have been very difficult to live with altogether, or maybe we just went house-to-house, shouting. No wonder there was a Civil War.

Talking to Jer on Livewhine

Thankfully, the wireless (and newspapers and the internet too, of course) was invented. And no Irish talk-radio show is ever short of contributors.

As a nation, we're not shy about venting publicly. Shy? We feckin' live for an audience to give out to.

We 'Talk to Jer'.

'Jer' is a kind of mash-up of the hosts of all the Irish talk-radio shows. He's greater than just one person and this is not any one particular show: Jer's on daytime, night-time, on shows you could call *Livewhine*. Sometimes the same people give out on all those shows (although double-moaning like that's not cool).

If Jer needs someone to give out yards to the nation, he won't be stuck.

Sometimes Jer is gentle and respectful; sometimes he takes on a more provocative persona, but ultimately he provides a national service – enabling Irish people to Give Out Yards in public. Jer gives us the rope. What we do with it is up to us.

Note: although Jer's presence will be felt here as the ear to every impassioned monologue, the reader of every letter and blog, we won't be hearing from him till much later. He's vital, but not important: it's the callers we're going to focus on. The ones actually doing the giving out.

They are our panel of experts. And so, let's . . .

Meet the Moaners

The best way to discover the heart of a nation is to find what they're Giving Out Yards about. And if the Irish have raised it to an art form, then some of us are full-blown Michelangelos. So, periodically, we'll be consulting some carefully selected fictitious expert givers-out: Seán the Religious Farmer, Máiréad Who Loves the Sound of Her Own Voice, Ciarán the Keyboard Warrior, Scamall de Spéir and Tom the Taxi Driver. This lot are peerless when it comes to peeves and they are not afraid to share them.

Seán the Religious Farmer

Meet Seán. Seán normally keeps himself to himself, but he has been known to write a letter to a local paper when something really gets his goat. Like the time that fella tried to get his goat (there's ongoing tension over a boundary hedge). He also lets his tongue loosen when he's had a few pints. He has great faith and is by no means a bigot: his best friend is 'Jim the Atheist'. They have some lively chats down in their local.

Seán inherited the farm and lived there with his mam until she died and he was forced to go speed dating to find a wife. He had tried online but realised most women like to be met first – albeit speedily – regardless of whether they are fit and strapping and perfect for the job. The speed dating was not a success, but on the way home from one particular session, he met a lovely woman on the bus. Actually, he already knew Betty from school, but back then he'd been too busy worrying that school was keeping him from the business of running a successful farm to notice her. Girls hadn't even been on the horizon back then. They got married in the local church – first time for both, so all above board.

Working on the farm and being close to nature only reinforces Seán's strong faith. He's a very nice man, even though he isn't much up for debating. He's fair, feels everyone should have a say, so he's more than happy to leave you at it. Unless he's had a few pints. Just ask Jim.

Máiréad Who Loves the Sound of Her Own Voice

Máiréad says she has her own private beliefs, but you wouldn't think they were private given how often she airs them in public. She's ambitious in her own way and tries to say what will get her ahead in certain quarters; this can mean she contradicts herself, depending on who's listening. She says, 'No, I didn't,' a lot when called out on the contradiction. She curses the internet for keeping a record of exactly what it was she said last year.

Máiréad doesn't always mention it, but she's high up in a think-group called Order of the Genitals (OOG). While you'll never be completely clear on what she really believes in private, you'll probably have a fair idea. You will, however, be absolutely certain of her opinion on everything else: from lunch to what birthing method you should use with 'hips like yours'. Máiréad just loves the sound of her own voice: as long as she sounds confident and manages not to swear, that's a win in her book. It's all about being out there: if Máiréad is giving out to as wide an audience as possible, she feels alive. She has the numbers of all the radio stations – local and national – on speed dial.

Some people have suggested that Máiréad should be a politician, but she doesn't want that at all. That would mean having to take action or be held accountable. People could then quite rightly give out about her. That simply isn't the point. If they do try to give out about her, she'll say 'As a mother . . .': her trump card. She thinks being a mother means she can say whatever she likes and, in fairness, a fair few people agree with this.

Máiréad is teetotal. She has to be on her contrary game at all times. She has weekly elocution lessons and speaks so clearly that many people think she's an alien. They also wonder whether the reason she's so patronising to anyone who disagrees with her is because she believes them to be base and primitive and it's for their own good. They're probably right.

Ciarán the Keyboard Warrior

Sadly, we've all met Ciarán online, but very few people have done so outside of the internet. Which is just as well because – not to put too fine a point on it – Ciarán's a dick. He very rarely leaves his house: he sees himself as one of those Wall fellas from *Game of Thrones*: eschewing human company to keep himself battle-fit and ready – agility of the mind trumps going outside. He doesn't exercise (duh) but he's had his best typing fingers insured. He made a few bob a few years ago from a game he helped design and the proceeds keep him in sweatshirts, snacks and pizza deliveries. Ciarán likes to say his blood type is 'cheese'. (Told you he was a dick.) Ciarán doesn't necessarily believe the stuff he spouts on forums or on Twitter (he was – according to himself – the third person in the world to join). He uses moaning like many people use *Sky Sports* – as a rainy-day hobby. He pokes wasps' nests when there's nothing else on. He achieved Wizard status on *Caves & Caverns* by day two – so all that's left for Ciarán is to stir things up in other people's lives.

When he really wants to give out yards, Ciarán uses the handle 'Slyfox99'; his avatar has amazing abs and pecs. They are not his own. He's doesn't care enough to hate, but he'll happily take whatever stance will get the best rise out of whoever he's engaging with today. Ciarán has been a big old Catfish on several dating sites, but never once shown up for a date IRL (in real life). Online, he did once kind of fall for Kiara in Killarney, and he has a rather large soft spot for Cody in Idaho. He would never admit this. He's a loner, keeps himself to himself, and lots of other stuff people say about serial-killers, except for the fact that serial-killers generally have to leave the house. But Ciarán doesn't know why you would. Not when someone can bring pizza *to him*.

Scamall de Spéir

Scamall leans so much to the left, you'd think she had a limp. 'Scamall' means 'cloud', and the name fits: she drifts from cause to cause with an ease that could suggest hypocrisy, were she not so damn sincere about it all. She rises at dawn every day, has a nice cool glass of freshly squeezed dew and as much of a shower as her rain-barrel allows.

The one thing she hates is the Man. Actually, she hates loads of things but she says, 'Love and light' a lot (it's the auto sign-off on her emails, so she doesn't have to type it every time). This means she has to pretend she's okay with certain stuff or she'd seem uncool. She is really, really angry. On her own behalf, for you, and for tons of people she hasn't met yet – but, make no mistake, if you need something shouted about, she has the megaphone. This isn't a metaphor; she has an actual bullhorn in the boot of her car. She would love not to have a car, but justice knows no county bounds, and she often has to drive to a protest. But the car runs on used vegetable oil she gets from her dad's chipper (he's very successful, which is why she can volunteer), so at least there's that.

Scamall pretends to be vegetarian 'to set a good example', but she's one of those who eats hot dogs when people aren't watching because, 'Sure, they're actually not even real meat anyway.' She sees herself as an artist, and one of her favourite forms of protest is to paint unflattering portraits of those she disagrees with and post them online. Then, for extra cash, she tries to flog them on Stephen's Green at the weekend.

Tom the Taxi Driver

Tom is a true-blue Dub. He has seen it all in the back of his cab, and knows it all as a result. Tom holds forth on world events and how everyone is doing everything wrong. If you get in Tom's cab, you're set for giving out for the day. You might emerge at your destination crying with laughter or seething with indignation, but one thing's for sure: you will have been schooled. It will give you something to think about, even if you vehemently disagree. Unlike Máiréad or Ciarán and their contrarian stances, designed to elicit a response, it doesn't bother Tom what you think. He only cares that you know what he thinks and so, if you're naive enough to reply, he'll only be half listening. He talks to himself when there's nobody there – you're just a prop.

Tom is his own boss and goes out to work when he pleases (as he's quick to tell you, freelancers 'like ourselves' work harder than anybody else) so he has the opportunity to see every televised debate and read every paper, if he chooses, although his favourite is station-hopping on the radio. Tom has heard or read everything before everyone else. Tom is professional – if he susses that your silence suggests disagreement, he will reluctantly dial it down: he has principles, but he still wants a nice tip.

He's the one the late-night talk shows can really rely on. Even if it seems like a topic that's a bit slow-news-day, Tom will be on it, like white on rice. Tom will deliver. Tom has an opinion on everything. And a nuclear bunker in his garden. He dug it himself in the late eighties.

And that's our crew! As we move through the topics, we'll be hearing from them occasionally. Whether we've asked for their input or not.

As Giving Out Yards is so important, so integral to Irish life, we're going to approach it scientifically. Alphabetically anyway. Kind of. The order isn't strict. (Something else to give out about there, if you like. Bonus!) They may not be the topics we most need to look at as a society – we do love to live in denial – but they are the ones that fascinate us again and again. The gifts that keep on giving out.

From A to Z, *Aborshhh…* to *Zygotes* (give or take the odd not-strictly alphabetical detour, for the craic), we'll see what most often makes Irish people come out in a rash and run straight past the calamine lotion to their laptop or phone.

Each topic gets a 'Moan factor' of 1 to 10, 10 being the most national-rage-inducing, 1 being a national blip – though, as we'll see, even trivial topics are worthy of giving out about. Let's face it, everything is.

And with that, we reckon you're prepped. Get ready to Give Out Yards.

Oh, wait. Before we do that, we should mention this:

What DON'T We Give Out About?

More than you'd think. These topics are either too much to handle in bite-size, giving-out chunks on the radio, or we're so used to them we don't even see them any more.

But here are just some of the things Irish people don't give out about:

* **Austerity**. So used to being shushened, we just went along with it. It's practically in our genes. Besides, we seem to feel that if we say the name too often, maybe we'll summon it. And it wasn't very nice.

* **Global warming**. We think this leads to nice summers. We'll do anything for one of those.

* **Global issues generally**. Do we know anyone involved? No? Then why should we care? We've enough nonsense to be dealing with at home.

* **Bad parking**. We agree. Spaces are hard to find. Sure, you'd have to go over the little white line. Don't worry about the rest of us, we'll drive around looking. It's a nice enough day.

* **Terrible customer service**. We're used to it so we don't expect much. You didn't poke us in the eye when you brought our dinner? You're getting a nice tip.

* **Litter.** Hard to say why we're so bad on this: we just don't seem to see it. No amount of Tidy Towns competitions can get it into our heads that, no, your fizzy drink can isn't biodegradable and, no, that isn't a bin. It's my handbag.

* **England**. We're much better buddies now. Anyone giving out about England or the English is hard up, when there's so much else to be giving out about.

* **Pain**. An Irish person's leg could be falling off and they will not give out about it.

* **Depression**. It's so widespread, there's a lot of empathy and compassion for this one. No giving out.

* **Privacy.** Ha! That's a good one. We don't have any. Knowing everything about each other's business is part of the Giving Out ethos.

NB: See *Ah, here* for suggestions on how to put up a conversational roadblock if you want to stop someone giving out about something.

Don't worry. Even eliminating these topics still leaves us with plenty to give out about. So let's begin.

★

Giving Out A-Z

A is for . . .

Aborshhh . . .

★ Don't say the A-word ★

Because in Ireland we're all Catholics, even those of us who aren't (more on that in *The Bongs! The Bongs!*), it's tricky to discuss reproductive rights here at all. But this topic comes up so often, and so shoutily, that we might as well get it out of the way early on or we'll all be fighting for the rest of the book and we'll never even get to G.

The thing is, we don't have aborshhh . . . in Ireland. We don't! So don't even say the word or the shouting will start. Definitely don't mention the ten to twelve women who go to England every day for the medical care they need. They're invisible! Do you really want to be the one who stops us believing in magic? Of course you don't. So, shhh. You and your facts.

Anyway, because we're all Catholics (even those of us who aren't), we're relatively new to discussing basic contraception, let alone the fact that we might actually not be damned for all eternity every time we unroll a condom for the craic.

But even still, only men are really allowed to have the craic, especially when it comes to sex. Women have to take it all very, very seriously because we are – if the establishment were honest – supposed to get pregnant every time we have intercourse over the course of our entire lives. Yes, all three to five times. And when you do get pregnant, well done: now you're a real Irish woman. That's it. No discussion.

It doesn't matter if this wouldn't have been your choice, if you're not in a position to parent, or if the pregnancy might not work out for some reason, we repeat: IT DOES NOT MATTER. Be happy! Put on your smock and sing, like some kind of expectant Snow White! Cop on to yourself and do your duty because, like we're always being told by people like Máiréad, 'Life is full of suffering.' For women anyway. Let's hear more:

★

Máiréad called *Livewhine* that time the foetus got the lawyer:

'I think women are brilliant – I'm one myself after all. I'd never fight a woman. And, as a mother, I'm in a position to dictate what's best for all women. They may think that it's all a bit of fun, Jer, having sex all the time with everyone they meet, but a child will soon put a halt to their gallop. That's why women get pregnant: it's nature's way of stopping our nonsense. I mean, a bit of sex is nice but you can't be having it your whole life.

'Some people don't feel cut out to be mothers but you know what'll sort them out? Motherhood! (Laughs.) They just don't know it yet. It will be the best thing I ever wanted to happen to them.

'And if they're worried a pregnancy won't go to term? It will. I'm telling you. It will. And there are loads of things you can do to distract yourself. If you go out for nice walks or make your own clothes or something, the nine months will only fly by. Life's awful. A bit of horror builds character and gives you a great standpoint from which to judge others.

'As for this new-fangled idea that a woman should choose what happens to her body? Ha-ha-ha! Who has that kind of choice? Who has that?

Sure, you could go under a bus when you leave here, Jer. I could give you a quick push and it'd be all over. Would you have chosen that? No. So if you don't have that right, Jer, why should women? Now I have to go, I've a clinic to picket.'

Two minutes later, Scamall called to respond:

'Jer, I can't believe that lady. I make all my own clothes and that has nothing to do with it. How can she say what's right for me, or anyone else? I mean, if she's so interested in my reproductive system, I'll give her my calendar and I'd be happy to let her buy my tampons for me. Although, to be honest – which I always am, I'm that kind of person – I'd prefer a Mooncup.'

They can give out at each other all they like; as with the best of giving out, it solves nothing. Irish women are getting on planes today. Or buying pills online, which could get them fourteen years in prison. Orange is the new crap.

But let's not dwell: even the government has admitted that they're 'sick of talking about it'. Sure, we know, lads! We know.

So, Ireland is lovely and pregnancy is always lovely and don't ever say the A-word. If you stick your head far enough into a sandpit, it's amazing what you can block out. Ireland is one big sandpit. And we all have ostrich-length necks.

Moan factor: 10

Fine Arse

★ Booty is in the eye of the beholder ★

This is usually what you'll be sitting on when you deliver your complaint about *Aborshhh* . . . or anything else. And you will be sitting: getting to your feet would be teetering dangerously close to action. Sit down and save your energy for giving your moan extra welly: more adjectives, that kind of thing. You don't want to waste any giving-out power through physical exertion.

Irish women aren't the only ones to bemoan the size of their arses, even though they're all perfect in their own way. If there's a sock for every shoe, there's definitely an arse-appreciator for every kind of posterior. But women all over the world moan about their arses, like the magazines tell us to, so Irish women aren't about to be left out. There's just more focus on ours than on the lads' – maybe we should focus on theirs a bit more. You know, for research? Because there's no doubt arses have got confusing and require further looking into. Or looking at, at least. Let's not go crazy.

Giving Out Yards

It used to be that certain arses were deemed 'too big'. Now the Kardashians seem to have inspired a kind of arse – we're not sure, they're so amazing, are they implants? – that everyone's supposed to have and arses just can't be big and round enough. Fake boobs out front, fake arses out back: if you think about it, given how precariously high heels are these days and how prone to falling this makes us, it's actually really smart padding. If you fall over, you just bounce right back up. Have you ever seen a Kardashian wriggling on the ground like an upturned tortoise? Of course you haven't.

On the rare occasion someone gives out about a lad's arse, it's usually because too much has been revealed – i.e. the dreaded builder's crack. A man comes to fix the sink, leans into it, and even if it doesn't quite end up in a bad soft-porn scenario, you still end up feeling you've learned a lot more about him than you might have chosen.

Ciarán, confused as he is by dealings with actual, real humans and wanting to explore these feelings in a creative way while still giving out yards, wrote this after he had his tap fixed last week.

★

BUILDER'S CRACK[*]
a poem by Ciarán

Drip, sink; drip, drip
What time do you call this?
I have been in all morning but will say I should be out
You've kept me in, you've let this drip, drip,
dripsplishy drop, plip-plop
Till I can't hear my thoughts think
Everything but the kitchen sink
And now you come with toolbag full and trousers low
And nothing about taps that you don't know
You bend to the U-bend, turn attention there
My eyes cannot escape the brilliant glare
Full moon over waistband
Much too low
Like, what you had for breakfast is on show
You wrench your wretched wrenching, drips no more
I plant my gaze now firmly on the floor
No, there will be no tip.

Brilliant, Ciarán, brilliant.

'Arse!' is also a handy way to give out in itself: an exclamation leaving no one in any doubt of your opinion on what's happened. You can use it in various ways:

---

[*] Technically, this is about a plumber, but Ciarán is big on poetic licence.

'That's arse!'; 'Arse biscuits!'; 'What a load of old arse.'
Or our favourite: 'Yer man is a total arse-wipe.'

Moan factor: 3.5/10

Ah, Here ... Put Giving Out on Pause

In case, even at this early stage, you're already overwhelmed
with the giving out, there's an A that buys you a breather.
Or it can be a stand-alone complaint, in itself: 'Ah, here.'

'Ah, here . . .' can mean:

1. 'Really? That's not how I perceive it.'

2. 'Feck off, that's a lie.'

3. 'Stop talking now, I'm bored.'

4. 'The football's on.'

5. 'Are you women still rabbiting on about
   aborshhh . . .?'

Anything you like. Just accompany it with a sneer and an
incredulously arched eyebrow.

If anyone gives out in your vicinity and you disagree
with what they're saying, just 'Ah, here ...' them. Game over.

But you don't have to limit yourself to 'Ah, here.' There
are plenty of silencing tools – like the contraptions they
used to put on guns in seventies cop shows, but seem to
have gone out of fashion. Nobody cares who hears who
shooting, nowadays.

There are many other great ways to stop people giving out about a topic you don't like, or have had enough of . . .

Just say, 'JOBS.' Everyone uses 'jobs' as an excuse for bad behaviour or as a distraction tactic. N.B. The tourism industry gets an extra special nod here.

Politicians' greed, our overreliance on tourism, the swapping of a beauty spot for a golf-course, just say, 'JOBS,' and no further elaboration is needed. You don't even need a full sentence, just 'But JOBS'. Job done. You'll see this in use again and again throughout the book.

Ditto 'They were different times.' Also known as 'tradition', as in 'Because tradition . . .'. Somehow this is magically supposed to excuse all kinds of awful. Say someone doesn't like the idea of a goat being up a scaffold for three days, and they happen to mention it aloud instead of silently thinking about goat welfare: gently shut them up by telling them it's tradition and asking why oh why do they hate Killorglin? They'll have to shut up then. Throw in 'they were different times' or 'it's just always been this way' whenever you need, and stop people in their tracks. You can't argue with the past!

Or say, 'As a mother', like Máiréad is so fond of doing. Everyone else is expected to stop speaking, genuflect and bring you a cup of tea. Nice.

'Only in Ireland!' Fast Forward Giving Out

If 'Ah here' shuts things down, saying, 'Only in Ireland!' does the opposite. It gives giving out a topper, a bit of extra polish. 'Only in Ireland!' ramps everything up. You'll either get everyone nodding in assent, or lynching you for lack of national pride.

Say, 'Only in Ireland!' about everything, even if it happens elsewhere and you know it.

'Only in Ireland!' somehow makes a complaint seem more handleable. You can take anything in bite-size green chunks. If something's 'only in Ireland' you could leave, if you chose, and put it behind you. You won't, though. Moaning about it is too much fun.

Tip: Accompany 'Only in Ireland!' with a sigh and an expert eye-roll and you're well on the way to not giving a shite about whatever the problem is.

NB: As with criticising someone else's iMOM* (Irish Mother or Mammy. And DON'T), it's probably best to make sure you've lived in Ireland for about thirty years before using this phrase.

Americans the Beautifuls

★ Are you for real? ★

To say our relationship with Americans is complex is an understatement. First, there's an implied aim that we're

---

* See *iMOM*.

all supposed to want to meet one, marry them, get a Green Card and get off the island immediately – so that's a lot of pressure if you ever have to date one. Or we're happy to stay here ourselves so long as they keep coming and buying Aran jumpers, taking tours of tin-whistle factories and teaching us about good customer service. They're usually really polite and lovely. So what's our beef?

Their enthusiasm. It kills us. It's too much. Like mole people exposed to too much sunlight, we're just not able for it and it makes us all squinty and unpleasant.

So, although Americans' souvenir-buying almost single-handedly brought the country back to life after the whole post-Celtic Tiger fiasco, we give out about them, too. We can't believe that anyone would sincerely wish anyone a nice day, when we know it won't be. We assume they're being insincere, even though we have absolutely no evidence of this. In other words, it's perfect giving-out fodder.

You can be said to be 'very American' or acting 'all American', which probably means you're being far too positive for your own good. Be very, very careful of that. Tone it down immediately by burying your face in an Aran jumper and copping on to yourself.

Moan factor: 7/10

★

B is for ...

The Bongs! The Bongs!

★ Give us this day our daily bells ★

This really is a great example of that aforementioned dark shadow of Dev and his buddy ABJCMcQ.

It's usually simplest for Irish people to agree that we're all Catholic, even those of us who aren't. It's what Dev and ABJCMcQ would have wanted and it just makes things easier, so kick back and go with the guilt-ridden flow. For those of you who aren't Catholic (you are, though), you probably don't even realise that there's a twice-daily reason for us all to give out: the Bongs.

Let's do this as quickly as possible: you see, the Angelus marks the Annunciation to Holy Mary by the Angel Gabriel that she was to have God's baby, without even checking if she'd a non-refundable holiday booked in the next nine months or anything. Luckily, she hadn't and she was up for it, despite not having met God before. She kindly overlooked His unwillingness to stick around in any kind of hands-on, holy nappy-changing kind of way, and luckily she had the support of her family – not to mention a ridiculously patient fella named Joseph.

Joseph married her and helped raise the baby before helpfully disappearing once God – like a rock star on tour – came back into the frame. (Incidentally, this kind of marriage would never have happened in the Ireland of The Shushening – Mary would have been spirited away to England, or to fluff 'n' fold convent sheets, while Jesus would have been sold to an American family and probably been a holy lawyer or something. But I digress.)

To commemorate this (Blessed) mother of all angelic pregnancy tests, bells in Catholic churches bong eighteen times twice a day, at midday and six p.m. The devout stop whatever else devout they're doing to be even more devout and reflect and pray. And fair play to them.

But what has some people up in arms is having the Angelus bells bonging away on the national, licence-fee-funded airwaves – radio and TV – in their kitchens, their living rooms or when they're already livid in traffic. Others are up in arms that they're up in arms. Some people oppose any religious iconography being used by a state broadcaster; some are angry at the favouring of just one religion's symbols, when loads more people in Ireland than ever aren't Roman Catholic (even though they are). Some of us aren't devout – or we are, but we're devoted to something else altogether, like disco. Some of us have an aversion to bells.

Pausing for the Angelus means the six o'clock *News* actually starts at a minute past six and has had to be renamed the *Six One News*. This drives some people straight to the disco for some angry dancing. The rest don't mind when the News happens. It will be bad. (See *The News*.) We can wait.

Some argue we should delete the bonging altogether, start the news on time and let people worship after their own fashion in their own homes or seething in cars. There are plans for the broadcaster to make the visual accompanying the bongs more secular: already it shows trains, waterways, people staring at trains and waterways. But even if they put it on with a picture of the most secular thing in the world – Donald Trump toupee shopping or something – whether you like it or not, some people just can't get down with the bonging.

Obviously, the Catholic Church has been the subject of some scary revelations that Dev and ABJCMcQ would really rather we'd skip over. Even fans of theirs, however, could live without being reminded of the scary revelations when they're having their tea. Many agree that scary tea is no tea at all. But it doesn't seem to be going away. And so, we give out about it. Or give out that people are giving out about it. Ireland may be moving out of the shadow of some scary stuff. The Angelus doesn't care – it just keeps bonging away in the background.

Moan factor: 10/10

★

Máiréad has had enough. She wrote to the paper:

Dear Sir,

I was listening to a 'comedian' on a television programme the other day, referring to the Angelus as 'bonging' and generally making a laugh out of it. As a mother, it made me very upset. My children love bells.

Each to his own and all the rest of it, but this kind of silencing of bells has got to stop. What next? Climbing into our houses at night and ripping the timers off our microwaves? Banjaxing our alarm clocks? Tearing down the steeple at Shandon, brick by brick? What else would Cork tourism have left, then? Blarney's miles away. It's a slippery slope. And a disgrace. It's a disgraceful slippery slope.

I love bells and they have only good connotations for me and my children. I don't want the bells to go, so they shouldn't. I've had it with 'comedians' thinking it's 'cool' to attack me personally, the same as if they came at with me with a 'big knife'. I'm terrified into silence and that's why I'm writing this.

'Comedian' is it? That's a joke.

Yours (delighted with herself for that one)

Máiréad

Black Fellas

★ Well, I've never seen one, Jer ★

This really is taking us a while to get our heads around, isn't it? Some of us still seem to get an awful fright when we encounter anyone living here who isn't ghostly pale.

In fact, some Irish people seem to believe people of colour only landed here early in 2015 when that lovely Timi fella had the @ireland Twitter account for the week. *A black fella being Ireland on Twitter? Wow!*

It was almost as if they didn't have windows or never went into town.

Older generations thought black people only came in size small, on the 'Black Babies' charity collection boxes in every shop and school. Or else they lived in America playing basketball or living it up in Bel Air, rapping and Fresh Princing at every opportunity. But we didn't have them here.

Guess what? That meant we didn't have racism! No! We didn't have that here. Ireland was a beacon to the world for its unique lack of racism. True, we also had a unique lack of people of colour, but let's not focus on that. And you'll be relieved to hear that now that we do have racism, we actually still don't have it at all! So how do we manage to give out about it?

Here's how: anyone highlighting racism wants to destroy Ireland. That's right. If someone suffers abuse or reports an incident they've witnessed, they're only 'looking for attention'; the giver-out has 'lived here much longer than you and never seen any racism happening. To anyone. Ever. So YOU are the problem.' They believe they're inclusive because if they have something bad to say about a person of colour (or someone from farther up the road than the bit they're used to) they'd 'never say it in front of them'.

So now you know. If you want to keep racism at bay, give out yards about the people giving out about it. It's a simple system but it works beautifully.

Moan factor: 0/0 because we don't have racism here

Seán was up in town once and he met a black fella. Back in his local, he told the story to Jim the Atheist.

'After the speed dating, I'd usually take the Luas to my train. But this session went mad late. I'd to get a taxi instead. I stuck up my hand, and the car pulls in, and who was driving it only a black fella?

Now, I'd talk to anyone, so I got in. I wanted to tell him he'd a lovely tan, but I was after reading somewhere that you're not supposed to. But he did, though. Lovely tan.

'Well, wasn't it the right land I got when he'd an

Irish accent. And he knew where the train station was. Says I, "You're Irish? I thought you'd be from somewhere more exotic, like the East!" Says he, "I am from the east: East Wall."

'Well, we'd a great old laugh after that. He's into the GAA and he likes Irish music. He'd never heard of Brendan Shine, though. Luckily, I'd a CD in my backpack so I gave it to him. Lovely fella.'

See also *Racist*.

Beards

★ Best hairy face forward ★

Remember when it was just Liam Ó Maonlaí and Gerry Adams who had the beards? And now look. They're everywhere! Just when we were getting the facial-recognition technology up and running, too. It's practically useless now.

Moan factor: 3/10

The Black and Tans

★ Target practice makes perfect ★

You couldn't class people's reaction to these scamps as mere giving out. In case you haven't heard of them, these feisty rapscallions were sent over from Britain during the War of Independence to fight the old Irish Republican Army. They were so great at fighting and killing and burning and stuff, they sometimes just kept doing it, even in their spare time, maybe even at a match. Well, you never get good if you don't practise!

The rumour is that some of them were released from prison to come and have target practice here. Even if that rumour isn't true, we should be proud of ourselves. We were a tough aim and became experts at running and hiding.

No moan factor here – too brutal. But it does highlight the fact that historical moaning is one of our favourite kinds: as seen in *Ah, here*, you can't argue with the past. But it'd be unwise to dwell on the B&Ts for fear of making people burst spontaneously into hours and hours of rebel songs and setting things on fire, which is what usually happens when you mention them.

However, they're included here partly because that reaction is not dissimilar to that now provoked by the next lads . . .

Banks

★ The 'W' is silent ★

This topic tips us over from casual givers-out to full-on professional rage machines. Like our friends above, these lads also mercilessly targeted civilians. We can feel good giving out about them.

Once upon a time, all a young school-leaver wanted was a job in the bank. You got to work in a nice dry building, wear a nice dry suit, you got loads of days off even though – as far as the rest of us knew – you only worked till three, and you got to count money every day until you retired. Lovely, lovely money, like all bankers love. The job was solid, dependable, decent. But in 2008, that all changed.

When the bold boys in Anglo Irish Bank made off with the lovely money of the entire country, the deed was done. Banks, and anyone who worked in them, became Public Enemy No. 1. Those suits aren't so dry now, are they?

Nowadays, only the worst kind of people work in banks. 'Banksters', some call them. That's one of the kinder epithets. They might be perfectly nice outside of work but, once in the bank, you couldn't trust them. Even someone who paints the outside of a bank risks being tainted by bankiness. Like the B&Ts, soon there'll probably be drinks named after them and songs about how they ruined the country. They won't be good songs.

Another B word never to utter aloud: BAILOUT. In a country that's fond of swearing (see *F-Bombs*), since the austerity we don't like to mention either, this word will forever be taboo.

Tom in his cab:

'I haven't been into a bank since 2008. Crooks, they are. Criminals. As bad as a murderer, nearly. Well, maybe not murder, but you wouldn't put it past them. You wouldn't be surprised if you found that out.

'When you go into a bank now, first someone trips you up and kicks you in the eye. Then they turn you upside down and shake every penny out of you. Then there's the bit of torture and more kicking in the eye. Then they show you an ad for themselves that starts by itself, even though you didn't ask it to play. That's worse than the torture, to be honest. Then they make you do a pub-crawl against your will and you have to foot the bill for them and all their mates. You do! I heard it! You know why so many people are banking online? Do you? It's cos they don't want to be kicked in the eye. No word of a lie.'

If Tom's attitude is representative (and it is) it's easy to see why even an ad for a bank can make us very cross:

Twinkly music, beautiful people. 'Come in,' they promise, 'we're not robbers and we won't kick you in the eye! Have a cup of coffee with Maureen the Manager (who's a human woman) and grab a mortgage on your way out. Without even getting a kick in the eye!'

But we're not fooled. We know that while Maureen the Manager might once have been human, she was relieved of her humanity the day she got that dry dark blue suit and kind-of-scarfy thing she wears because she's been told it makes her look more approachable. Come off it, Maureen. Give us some credit. NOT THAT KIND. We're already massively in debt.

They'd be far better off with more honest bank ads:

No music. No set. No nothing. 'Hello! We're a bank. If you take out a loan, we will definitely be kicking you in the eye at some stage. But you need us. So take it. Take your kicking.' *KICK.*

At least then we'd know where we stand.

Moan factor: 9.75/10

Babies

★ Lower your expectations ★

Babies are lovely. Everyone loves babies, right? Unless you're on a plane or in a restaurant. Then they're the devil's spawn but *so cute*. If you're in a restaurant or plane with a baby, don't waste the opportunity to split the country. Call *Livewhine* straight away and let Jer have it about how your lunch was ruined by a spoiled brat. You will soon be joined on the line by about a thousand people defending the baby, saying, 'It's only a baby', which might be true in the strictest sense, but no help at all getting out drool stains or relieving shriek-induced tinnitus.

You would think, with this sort of auto-baby-defence outcry, that Ireland would be very pro babies. It is not. Oh, sure, before they're born they can have a full legal team. But when someone's actually been born, they have to sort themselves out sharpish. You can't expect your parents and the state to do everything – have you seen the cost of childcare? Irish parents pay the highest childcare costs in Europe and grandparents won't be around for ever to pick up the slack. Grandparents in Ireland are doing their best to live longer just so there's someone to babysit. Soon only the wealthiest will be able to afford offspring and the rest of us will die out. Do you want the future of the country to be descended from bankers? Is that what you want? Come on, babies! Get a job!

It was easier in the old Shushening days, when you could just put babies straight to work or sell them to the highest bidder in America. One more fistful of dollars, one less potential restaurant-experience-ruiner.

Those really were the days, alright.

Moan factor: 5/10

Breasts

★ Hidden assets ★

Babies lead us nicely on to breasts, which should be pleasant things to be led on to.

But they cause consternation in this country. First, women insist on getting them out IN PUBLIC to feed the aforementioned babies in a totally natural way (with no mind to who might be offended by this outrageous natural occurrence). Not only that: loads of women seem to have them *just for fun*. They have the audacity to wear them out front, all up in people's faces. What the hell is going on there?

Breasts, as we all know, should be strapped down in shame in the hope that everyone will forget about them. Better yet, could you not conceal them under some kind of habit? That would be best for everyone.

NB: You are allowed to discuss breasts if you are a cancer survivor. In that case, Ireland is pretty great and supportive, like a big green padded bra. Other than that, though, remember that breasts are shameful and too directly connected to the dreaded S-E-X to have any place in a decent society.

Moan factor: 34C/10

★

Blasphemy

★ A taste of medieval times, today! ★

Yes! Even in 2015 we have this to give out about. Not only is everyone in Ireland Catholic – all together now: 'Even those of us who aren't' – but there seems an extra super-duper souped-up suspicious Catholic cabal, with spies everywhere (possibly Dev and ABJCMcQ's henchmen), waiting for you to take the Lord's name in vain or not bow your head when you're passing a church or something. Once upon a time, the head-bowing was probably a joyful manoeuvre of worship. Nowadays, with all the scary stuff that's gone on, it's hard not to detect a little nod to The Shushening in it, and you rarely see people bowing any more. But this makes the super-duper souped-up ones very annoyed.

There's finally a move towards a more secular Ireland, keeping Church and state apart, but you have to be careful if you propose this separation because (*whispers*) it is blasphemy, and we have a law against it. Now, it's not clear what happens if they catch you blaspheming on your own time, but no one's ever reported back after being caught and that can't be a good sign. If you blaspheme at work, though, or anywhere you might be overheard and seen to be spreading your blasphemy, watch out.

The worst thing about the blasphemy law is that, although it may sound medieval (the kind of thing Henry VIII would impose because somebody didn't like his hat), the latest version came into effect in 2009. That's no laughing matter.

Even if you have a sincerely held belief that God has a sense of humour, you must definitely not make jokes about Him. If you come up with a joke about The Big G, even a great joke, you could be fined €25,000 for the laugh. Comedians don't have that kind of money, so they tend not to do that kind of joke. The Shushening is long gone. Not.

Last night in his local, Seán had a suggestion:

'Why don't we bring back stocks? There's no point fining broke people! As far as I'm concerned, the Lord's well able to take a joke. But if He's not, wouldn't stocks be cheaper, and sure don't comedians only love being laughed at? If we're going to go medieval, let's do that.'

Ah, here.
Moan factor: €25,000/10

Balance

★ We don't know when to stop ★

In the East, they have the whole balance thing down. *Yin* and *yang*, sweet and sour, darkness and light. Here in Ireland, we still don't quite have the hang of it.

We don't do moderation here AT ALL. You're either drunk or dehydrated. Feasting or famining. Kicking people in the eye or a debtor with a sore eye. Something about the middle ground freaks us out: we want to get as much as we can of a thing and then to punish ourselves for the over-indulgence. We have great bouts of national FOMO (Fear of Missing Out, for those who don't enjoy the internet), followed by great big dollops of guilt. Lent is *huge* here. It's like a forty-day detox we think will make everything okay.

A mad extension of this not-quite-'getting' balance is that you cannot debate a topic on the Irish airwaves unless you have someone to counter it. Opposite ends of the same giving-out, basically. For and against, timed with stopwatches even when the issue is a human right. We know this sounds like stocks time again, but this is how it is. Everyone gets to give out.

'I think racism is bad.'

'Thanks for that. Now we have John Goodoleboy from the Ku Klux Klan to give his reasons why lynchings are a perfectly civilised way to spend a Friday night.'

Though we're all for everyone having their say, it's a little tedious constantly having to hear out people like John. He's so hard to hear through his sheet.

Moan factor: 4/10

Battle of Battenberg

★ Cake camps: which side are you on? ★

Not strictly a national concern, but the topic has brought more Cork* families to blows than *Balance* or *The Bongs* combined.

Battenberg is a cake. BUT WHICH CAKE? The square marzipan-covered yellow-and-pink one? Or is it the triangular chocolate-covered brown-and-yellow one? Well? Admit it, you know which *you* think it is, but you're afraid to say. It's terrifying.

Listen long enough to a local Cork radio station and the question will come up. It just will. There are cousins who haven't spoken since the seventies because of a teatime altercation, one party feeling tricked by the name, disgusted at the appearance of the 'wrong' cake, the other proclaiming their rightness through mouthfuls of mostly yellow crumbs. Important: they may both be wrong. No one has ever been able to verify any of this scientifically. All we have are anecdotes: terrible, tragic, cake-related anecdotes.

Ciarán has no time for any of this. He once went to his auntie's house in Cork for tea against his will and tried to set his cousins straight:

---

* We're sensing mass giving-out occurring almost countrywide: 'Cork? Why a Cork-specific topic? What's so special about Cork?' We'll deal with this in *Corkistherealcapital*.

45

'Dudes: they both taste the same. And you can't cut either of them without them turning to sawdust. They're supposed to have distinct ingredients, but they don't. So what you're left trying to do is taste colours. I mean, like, if your tongue can't distinguish between yellow and pink, you're screwed, because there are no other flavours in there.'

Ciarán's auntie started crying and he hasn't been asked back to tea since. Which suits Ciarán. He's more of a cheese man.

Moan factor: Yellow. Maybe pink. No, brown!/10

It's surprising that more people from the rest of the country haven't spotted this method of dividing – and thereby conquering – Cork. Because, as we all know…

$\mathcal{C}$ is for . . .

Corkistherealcapital

★ Cork is the real capital ★

The real capital. The Rebel County. People not from Cork don't like people from Cork, but Cork people know it's just jealousy. Probably because they're afraid of their awesome power. Yes. It must be that. Boi.*

---

* Full disclosure: the author is from Cork.

What the haters can't possibly know is what it's like to grow up in a place where you know you're the best but literally nobody else will acknowledge it. Where you've to defend yourself over cake (see *Battle of Battenberg*). Where you have some of the world's most beautiful scenery but Americans only seem interested in having a jaunting car take them from Shannon to Killarney, bypassing you completely. Thank goodness someone invented Shandon and the Blarney Stone or we'd *really* have had to start acting out for attention.

It doesn't help that everyone takes the piss out of the way we, speak, either: you're either 'too Cork' or 'not Cork enough'. If every sentence doesn't go up and down like a game of linguistic snakes 'n' ladders, many will doubt your heritage. If you do the beautiful singsong we all know and love, people from outside the county snigger – even if you're delivering a eulogy or speaking in your capacity as head of a political party.

Cork people are well able to give out about anything, but what really hurts us – what we'd love to get off our chests, if only we felt safe enough – is the daily prejudice encountered as a direct result of being born in Cork. It is a grave injustice to be hated before you even open your mouth and then ridiculed when you do. Stop silencing us. Stop the hatred. We can't help being powerful and brilliant. Boi.

It's hard to discuss Cork without giving a shout out

to another C and one of its most famous sons: Michael Collins. Basically, you're either a fan of the 'Big Fellow', or you're not. You may have seen him in a film where he was Liam Neeson, who is very tall. Well, legend has it that MC was twice Neeson's height and far more likely to win an Oscar. On the other hand, you get people giving out about his selling six counties for thirty pounds of silver flesh, or something.

The Ireland of Collins might have been a very different Ireland from the one under Dev and ABJCMcQ; possibly not so Shusheningy and definitely better dressed. He totally rocked hats. But luckily for them, he died young. Luckily for him, he died in his native Cork, which hopefully made up for all the having to lie in ditches and carry messages in his socks during his lifetime.

Moan factor: Boi/10

Crime

★ A topic we love to hate ★

No matter what county you're from, bad guys are sexy. Even with that in mind, though, Ireland's gone cray-cray for the crime recently. We know we shouldn't, but we seem to really fancy crime. We know it's bad, but we absolutely love giving out about it. When even Spike Island (a former correctional facility) is an adventure camp, it shows you our fun attitude to crime these days.

No one seems to agree more on the sexiness of crime than the Irish tabloid press and our most sensationalist documentary makers. Has there been a shooting? They'll have a sexy picture of it or a sexy interview with someone who saw the whole sexy thing. Has there been a big sexy robbery, preferably at sexy gunpoint? Let's judge the people who've been robbed (sexily) if we possibly can. And if a woman has had the misfortune to be the victim of a crime, SHE'S NICKED: as far as they're concerned, she did it. She certainly asked for it. Silly woman. No full-page interview for her.

If crime went away, the rest of giving out wouldn't be half as sexy: we'd only be left with the rain, and stuff like that. It doesn't help that *Love/Hate*, Ireland's biggest TV drama in recent years, was quite as successful as it was. Maybe that's *why* it was. It felt familiar, like we were going just under the surface of the actual news. All it was missing was a reporter between the gritty scenes, summing things up to camera and wondering whether Eastern Europeans might have been involved. (We love nothing more than a good old-fashioned scapegoat. Irish people can be really lovely to each other if we've someone else to moan about.)

And, let's face it, our justice system is just weird (more in *Judges*). It's the best craic. Fellas get suspended sentences because they've businesses in town or are 'too attractive' to be able to clear their licensed premises. Foetuses get lawyers.

Homosexuality was illegal here until the year Al Pacino won a Best Actor Oscar for *Scent of a Woman*, and 'Whoomp! (There It Is)' topped the charts (1993, trivia fans), and that's only yesterday as far as most of us are concerned.

But the fun thing is that we get to give out not just about sexy crimewaves and sexy criminals but about what actually constitutes a crime in the first place. It's not always what you'd expect! As every caller to every radio station in the land will tell you: 'There's no justice, Jer.'

Moan factor: 7/10 (men), 10/10 (women)

Censorship
★#REDACTED ★

Robotic voice: 'There is no censorship in Ireland. Repeat: there is no censorship in Ireland.'

We're all free to say whatever we like so long as it's the right thing. According to whom? Whoever has the snazziest lawyer, of course.

We're free, except for the threat of great big lawsuits if you disagree with certain quarters or call them out, or whatever. It's amazing how the threat of a suit – no matter how ludicrous – can shut down individuals and organisations. Really effective. We must try it sometime.

For a while there in 2015, it felt like everything everyone said was *# redacted*, even if you were only in the post office, asking for stamps. 'Redact that there, Séamus,' you'd say. 'It wasn't the air-mail rate I wanted at all.' It's not clear whether if we're using the word 'redacted' correctly just yet, but we're following what examples we have.

So, there is no censorship in Ireland, despite what radicals say in interviews or online. Not really. It's surprising those radicals haven't been sued yet. But that's probably only a matter of time.

Moan factor: Shhh/10

Ciarán, posting on a forum as SlyFox99:

Don't tell me I'm wrong – that game is useless. Useless. It's not a matter for disagreement, it's fact. STOP SILENCING ME, FASCISTS!!! I'll redact your ass so fast . . .

Cyclism

★ Life in the not-so-fast lane ★

Cyclism: the irrational hatred of cyclists. Like racism or sexism but aimed at two-wheelers. (*Yes, we know some of them are annoying but come on, now.*)

Tom in his cab:

'You see those bike couriers? You wanna know their life expectancy on the streets of Dublin?' *Snaps fingers.* 'That.'

For 'invisible' road users, cyclists sure do generate some great giving-out and they really keep Jer and his colleagues busy moaning on *Livewhine*. On a bike, you may not be invisible, but you certainly feel as if you are. You can high-vis the legs off yourself, string all kinds of flashing lights from your rear mudguard to front spokes, yet the experience of the average cyclist is one of being completely transparent. Every other road user will still say you're nothing but a hazard and that cyclists are hell-bent on using their powers of invisibility to wreak evil havoc on everyone else.

People speak of cyclists like pigeons: if they weren't so beneath them, they'd have put them in pies long ago. That said, with the givers-out being such busy people about town who can't slow down *for anything or anyone, ever*, I'd say a cyclist would take too long to cook. Besides, their calves would be quite tough.

Listen up now. You're not going to like this but at least it'll give you something to give out about: cyclists are vehicles too. Well, technically the bikes are, but you rarely see them out without a rider. Check out the *Rules of the Road*. And remember how delighted you were when the decision came in to fine them like everyone else who uses the road? Oh, you were so delighted. Well, just like the people of Cork, you can't have your cake and eat it too: it works both ways.

Bikes are vehicles. You have to let them do their vehicular thing. They're allowed to be at a traffic light, ahead of you. They're allowed to make a right turn. They aren't allowed to be nuisances and cycle on pavements, but let's let the fines take care of that, shall we? You can drop the indignant vigilante act now. Because bike-human combos are vehicles that also happen to be people.

It may surprise you that something that has the life expectancy of a fly, or – *snaps fingers* – 'that', is actually a real-life human, but there you go. Just because they irritate you doesn't mean you can swat them. They can be squooshed. You, Annoyed Person in a Lorry, will win. And you probably won't feel so good about the swatting then.

Some cyclists give us all a bad name: darting in and out of traffic, sneaking up on the inside of vehicles mid-turn, or performing wheelies on the M50 when they're not supposed to be there in the first place. And they should be fined. In fact, seven more fines were brought in recently. Well, that was the announcement made recently to the glee of motorists nationwide, but strictly there's just one: €40, covering seven offences. So we get it, we behave badly in traffic and we can be fined like the rest of you. But don't let a few genuinely bad two-wheeled apples colour your view of the rest. They may be bad apples, but they don't deserve to be made into smoothies.

The Antelope Experience

If you ever want to really get a feel for the thrill of what it's like to be an antelope being pursued by a hungry, angry lion on an African plain, simply try cycling in a bus lane, like you're supposed to. A hungry, angry bus driver is almost guaranteed to tear after you, bearing down, engine roaring and trying to clip your rear quarters. You do your best to evade him, heart pounding, all flailing limbs, instinct and lactic acid, knowing that if he decides to finish you off, you're powerless. And wishing you'd brought a change of underwear. Best of all, the Antelope Experience is free! All you need is a bike, and the willingness to take your courage in both your sweaty hands.

It would be wonderful if Ireland were a safer place to be on two wheels. After all, they're our second most traditional way of getting around, after the John Hinde donkey and cart.

But it's just too much fun to give out about cyclists. Are we really ready to deprive the public of one of the last acceptable 'isms'?

Moan factor: 3/10

Giving Out Yards

Tom calls a late-nite talk show:

'I didn't even see him, Jer, he came out of nowhere. There he was, in all his neon gear, taking up the middle of the yellow box junction, hand out, turning right, bold as you like. But it was taking for ever, Jer, and I've a job to do. So I revved the engine a few times, you know, just to let him know I was there, like. And he turns and looks at me, all stressed and sweaty, like I'm annoyin' him. I've places to be, Jer! I've fares to pick up. If you're goin' somewhere on a bike it's not work, is it, Jer? That's a hobby, that is: you're certainly not in a hurry. Do you've a bike? Of course you don't. You're a businessman. He's probably just cruisin' around for the laugh, takin' up space and tonin' his calves, the neon eejit. So I beeped him. I gave him a good old blast of the horn, and he jumped and tried to turn into the oncoming traffic, the fool. Well, the traffic screeched to a halt and yer man skidded and came off the bike, and do you know what he did when he got up, Jer? He came over to me, knocked on the window, big red cross face on him. He looked like he'd hit me a dig so I told him to shag off. He was all right, wasn't he? He was up and his leg wasn't hangin' off. The bike was grand only it was in the middle of the road now. "Pick up your bike," says I, through the window. "You're holdin' up traffic." Well, the cursin' out of him! I couldn't repeat it here, Jer, I'm a gentleman and so're you, but let me just say that there was nothin' wrong with his middle finger anyway. That was workin' alright! They shouldn't be on the roads, Jer. Shouldn't be on the roads.'

Clamping Pain

★ Move it or lose it (your car) ★

This is a fantastic new enterprise in Ireland. So fantastic that it was not affected by the 2008 crash in any way. In fact, if anything, it grew. If you live in Ireland and you drive, at all, ever, you've been clamped. And a lot of people do drive, despite the expense. Well, you've seen how risky cycling can be in a society rife with cyclism.

People had very little spare change back in 2008, so once parked they pushed *to the limit* the 15-minute grace period between meter running out and getting back to their cars. Idiots.

They should have known who they were dealing with: not amateurs, that's for sure. They should have known how dedicated the clamping teams were, how very good at their jobs. Some workers slack off, leaving something half done because their hearts aren't in it. Not clampers. Clampers go all the way.

And they are rumoured to be freakishly strong: they can carry up to ten clamps in their magic trouser pockets and lift a 2001 Micra onto the back of a truck with their teeth.

Getting clamped and giving out about getting clamped are both inevitable, so to help you maximise your giving-out enjoyment, we've given you some reasons to be cheerful about clamping.

STANDARD CLAMPER GIVE-OUTS	THE BRIGHT SIDE OF CLAMPING
✳ They hover. They lurk with intent.	✳ Lurking in a high-vis jacket on Merrion Square in broad daylight is no mean feat.
✳ They 'cruelly' swoop in like vultures while you rummage for the last bit of change behind the front seat of your car.	✳ We say, admire the skill of the swoop while you rummage. The instinct! The speed! The consistency!

➡

* They know exactly how long a minute is, just by feel. And they know you're lying, both about how long you'll be gone AND the baby you just invented.

* You can't afford to park near your work any more, in case a job runs over.

* These dedicated soldiers force us to take a good hard look at ourselves and realise that someone out there is working harder and making more money than we ever will. Let it motivate you.

* You plead with them to let you park for two minutes while you run into a shop to pick up nappies and formula. Your pleas are blatantly ignored.

* They know you're really buying chocolate and the *RTÉ Guide*.

* You missed your gym class, waiting for them to come back and release you.

* You had to walk all the way home because you didn't have enough cash on you to get unclamped or hop into a taxi.

* They keep us fit by having us sprint back to where our cars used to be, one hot, useless fifty-cent piece held in front of us as we run. These legends even help us to appreciate the city by 'encouraging' us to leave the car at home, choosing bus, bike or feet over inconvenience, financial loss and humiliation.

* You resent giving them exorbitant fees for going a tiny bit over your time.

* JOBS!!! Saying this makes everything in Giving-out World okay. Even if someone's a tyrant, at least they're off the live register.

When it comes to clamping, it's always best to focus on the positive. And it's even better not to mess with anyone with such freakishly strong teeth.

Moan factor: 1/10–10/10, depending on the area/alertness of the hovering

Camping in the Streets
★ How to sleep tight when people are sleeping rough ★

Staying in that positive mode (though not for long, we promise), let's make like the government and reframe!

Sometimes, you need to give out – and not take action – about something that's really too terrible to contemplate. To take a terrible picture and make it look good. Hurrah!

(*Warning: heavy irony.*)

The great thing about us is how hospitable we are. Everyone's welcome! We're so friendly. Knowing your entire extended family, and having that knowledge stretch back for generations, means everyone really fits in and knows exactly where they belong. So that must mean that everyone has somewhere to stay and we don't have any homelessness! As with the racism, there's nothing to give out about here, if you just ignore some facts. Like the fact that there are over a thousand homeless kids in Dublin right now.

Back to that reframing. Everyone knows homelessness

is a terrible thing. In Ireland, at the moment, it's at a crisis point. So how do we live with ourselves, knowing it's not enough this time to give out on the radio or in the newspapers but do nothing, while still achieving the doing-nothing part? Let's play a fun reframing game we call *How Do We Sleep?*.

In front of your face	How do we sleep?
✳ You pass someone sleeping in the street. It makes you sad.	✳ They're just camping. You've seen the Tourist Board ads: people are forever going off in tents to see this beautiful country of ours. Well, imagine waking up with a stunning view of Leinster House or the Central Bank. Every day! Wow.
✳ But the people in the doorways don't have tents.	✳ They're hardy. Haven't they a grand sleeping bag and a grand doorway?

Breathe in that delicious bus-fume-filled air and you're guaranteed to have the sleep of your life. If your conscience is letting you sleep as well as they are, we'll be shocked.

* But who are they? Where do they come from?

* We have an answer for that. No one says it aloud, but how else are you going to sleep? They're bad people. Good people don't get up sleeping in the streets. Good families who work hard don't get into trouble and find themselves sleeping in cars. And don't forget: some people really love their cars and their kids. Who are we to deprive them of quality time with both?

* It can happen to anyone. It can happen easily.

* It's awful.

* Aren't there any strategies in place? It can't go on like this. The government funding never seems to arrive.

* Yes, but some people marry princes in the end! And Leinster House is made of cake! Cake for everyone!

* Yeah, but DRUGS. A lot of it's drugs. At least they're enjoying themselves. More than me, says you, hah?

* Of course. We wouldn't be able to sleep if we didn't think bright government sparks were on the case. One cool plan is to arrest people for homelessness. I KNOW! We can't believe the audacity either. But seriously, though, it would get

	those drug-addled campers off the streets in no time.
✳ You can't be serious.	✳ I know, yeah. Anyway, be careful to step over the legs of that person stretched across the pavement. Don't look down. You don't want to catch The Drugs off them.

Moan factor: 1/10 (Though we should be complaining about this one all day long)

𝒟 is for . . .

Dead Certainty

★ Nothing is certain but death and sandwiches ★

So, we reach the big one – Death. Irish people will discuss this issue pretty much every day until our own inevitable demise. We love to give out about it – partly because giving out about it reassures us that we're not currently having to do it.

We're huge fans of it and, of course, of giving out about it and all its paraphernalia. We're not fans of the passing of a loved one, of course. No one is a fan of that. But, in fact, sometimes the passing of someone we didn't get on with can be even worse: losing someone you've loved to give out about on a daily basis can leave you bereft in more ways than one.

Death gives us plenty to give out about: its coming, its failure to come fast enough, who might be next, where they'll be buried, who'll get the house. If we aren't thinking about our own deaths (and most of the time we are), we're speculating on those of others. But it's important to remember that even when we're focused on another's departure, it's really all about us:

1. **I'm** sorry they're dead.

2. **I'm** going to sit up at the front of the funeral mass.

3. **I** know the widow very well.

4. **I** only saw him yesterday and he was delighted to see me.

5. **I'm** not dead yet. Ha!

There are little old ladies down the country with bets running and dates marked out on Advent calendars of doom. They're rarely wrong. They're not just giving out: they're watching out. And soon, somebody will be paying out.

Death itself isn't the only thing up for giving-out grabs. The rituals get it in the neck, too:

* The flamboyance of the funeral: too flashy, and the family thinks they're great; too simple, they obviously couldn't give a feck.

* That was a very long mass. There's no need for it.

* The priest said the wrong name. In fairness, he'd never met the deceased because only a few people come along on a Sunday.

* The aptness of the site of the grave: 'That's not their family plot'; 'Is it a bit . . . sunny?'

* The freshness and variety of sandwiches. It's best to have some on brown bread in case an overseas cousin is a health nut. You can later give out about the trouble you had to go to, as a bonus.

* Who didn't bring any sandwiches? Forget the deceased, these losers are now dead to you.

* Someone brought pizza. They were never alive to you in the first place.

* 'They're getting cremated? Do they think they're American?'

* Was it a 'good death'? There's never been a *Good Death Handbook*,* so it's hard to be sure what one is but there's a lot of pressure to have one. We can only suppose it involves a whole heap of rosary-saying and sandwich-bringing.

* A bad death would probably be one where no one brought any sandwiches.

When we shake the hand of the bereaved, we say, 'I'm sorry for your trouble.' We avoid the word 'loss' in case it would remind them of what was really going on and set them off; in the flurry of sandwiches, we hope they've forgotten their bereavement. They'll only get upset if you don't distract them with bread. So distract them with bread, goddammit.

We downgrade bereavement – like the conflict in Northern Ireland – to 'trouble', a word you might use when you get a flat tyre on your way to the airport or you can't find your glasses because they're on top of your head. This downgrade also gives a neat message to the bereaved: DON'T GET ALL MESSY AND EMOTIONAL,

---

* If you know what a Good Death is, write the handbook: it'll only fly off the shelves.

PLEASE. No one can handle that. After all, this funeral is all about us.

> **Historical note:** because it was always all about us, we used to get professional *keeners* to do the crying at funerals. It meant we could get on with our real role in all this: keeping the relatives calm and criticising the wake . . . We mean, making more sandwiches.

The wake is usually such a joyous thing that it rarely elicits much giving out. Ha! Wrong. We never take compassionate leave from that. Enjoy the singing in the moment, keep the bereaved sandwich-focused, and conserve your energy for the next day. Then you can give out about how you'll have a much better wake when it's your turn, and all you ask of anyone coming to it is to cry. And bring a massive platter of sandwiches.

Moan factor: 6/10

> **From:** Seán McCarthy, Topfield Farm
> **To:** Black & Sons Undertakers
>
> *Dear Sirs*
> *As I write this, I'm feeling fine, so please don't take this as a sign that I'm going anywhere. I'm not. But if I do 'go'*

for any reason, I don't want my wife, Betty, to have to worry about anything. And I don't want anyone giving out about me after I'm gone, saying the do wasn't up to much. So I'm leaving you my plans, which I trust you'll carry out to the letter.

I do not want a fancy coffin with door-knocker-looking things on. I've never understood those yokes because the person inside is dead and wouldn't hear if you did knock. They're too flashy anyway. I would like my name on the box, to avoid confusion.

The box itself: the plainest one you have. I don't want anyone saying I thought I was great, in life or after it.

I will be sending Fr Murphy full Requiem Mass instructions, but I don't want to be carried in. I've never been carried and I'm not planning to start in full view of the public. Wheel me in, please. I'm a big lad, so if you need a wheeling mechanism, let me know. I've loads in the shed. But ask me sooner rather than later as after I'm gone, it'll be too late to consult on this.

No singing. Just prayers, thank you.

Flowers from the farm if summer. Nothing if winter. I used to have a thing about cremation. I thought it was too quick and all that. But I was burning the stubble the other day and I thought, it's as natural as the other way and maybe a bit less fuss. So I would like to be *cremated, please. My wife will know where the ashes should go.*

I think that's about it. Please send me a bill for the whole shebang ASAP so we're square in advance. I'll have left money for food (sandwiches, both colours) and drink at the local, so please call in yourselves. It'll have been a long day for you and I don't want ye or anyone else giving out I was tight.

Yours sincerely,

Seán

High Drama

★ Not quite Greek tragedy . . . but we hold our own ★

It's easy to assume that giving out without action is just about venting spleen. Not so. Here, we look a little closer at how the Irish really raise it to High Art. Giving out is nothing if not a massive outlet for our creativity.

We can make a drama out of anything:

* They've changed the aisles at your supermarket so you can't find the dried parsley, and you've people coming. Do a monologue about it for the next six weeks. Repetition alone – to your partner, friends, kid's teacher, talk-show host – will hone it to

Beckettian brilliance. The hundredth time you do it, make people pay in.

* Don't limit yourself. A bill has arrived, or someone in government has said something. Anything. Get your thesaurus out because you're going to need more than just 'disgusting' or 'disgrace' if the rest of the country's givers-out are going to take you seriously. Try 'travesty', 'sham' or 'unmitigated something or other'.

* No niggle is too small to make into a big drama.

* Take moral umbrage at everything. No one but you and the people who agree with you are right.

* Rend clothes, throw yourself to the ground, shake your fist at the sky – preferably outside the gates of Leinster House. Write poems, songs, make posters. Fly! Give out! Be free!

* Talk to Jer – and the rest of the country – before anyone else, including the emergency services.

* Go big or go home. Exaggerate. You didn't get a clip of somebody's bumper – YOU NEARLY DIED.

Make a moan out of anything and a meal out of every moan. We really are the best little country in the world for giving out creatively, all the same. Let's take a bow.

Moan factor: 2/10

Dáil Airin'

★ **That shower in Leinster House** ★

And speaking of Drama . . .

In fairness to our politicians, they give us plenty to give out about. They would test even a less moany nation. They really don't care! They don't even pretend! All the parties are exactly the same! So we're royally screwed – and 'royally' is apt because, with no alternative, we may as well have a king.

At least if we had a king, we might have some pomp and the odd fabulous wedding. Instead all we have is 'pump', of the parish variety, and very little ceremony at all.

Tom in his cab:

Tom: 'This lot are a shower. A rotten shower. And the other lot? A worse shower. I'm not voting for any of them.'
Passenger: 'So what are you going to do in the next election?'

Tom: 'Emigrate.'

He won't, of course: he'll stay and live-moan the whole campaign, like the rest of us.

Why do we let them off with so much? Why do we keep giving them our votes? Truth? We secretly admire their giving-out skillz. We'd be shocked if they suddenly *did* anything and would scamper away like startled rabbits.

Irish people used to vote for whoever their granddad knew in the pub or the first to get the pothole near our house fixed. So if the potholes aren't getting fixed and no one is telling the truth – even after a few jars – who do we vote for?

'Tell me your policy on X or Y,' you'll say to the handsome young fellas and young wans they put on posters now. On the doorstep, you tell them your hopes and fears for the country. But they aren't listening at all. They're thinking about their next teeth-whitening appointment: they've a poster shoot coming up. A poster shoot paid for by the taxpayer. You.

Scamall: 'Never trust a politician.'

But in Ireland, ironically, you can. Because you know they're lying. There's fantastic consistency there. And you can always trust an Irish politician for incredibly entertaining giving-out opportunities like:

* selling all our planes
* helping create and enforce fantasy water charges
* running up intercontinental personal phone bills
* maybe or maybe not having been in paramilitary organisations
* maybe or maybe not giving a tuppenny shit about women
* Pretending we've no room
* getting their teeth whitened but never smiling outside of poster time
* founding 'new' parties which are THE SAME
* founding 'new' parties which face the wrong way: backwards, towards 1950, just as Dev would have liked it.

Tom in his cab:

'Gobaloons! Shite, they're are. Pure shite! Would I vote for them again? Sure of course I would! The other shower are only trotting after them.'

You see, there's comfort in what we know. 'If they're not lying, how did they get in?' we ask. Possibly something involving naked pictures of someone from the other shower and, let's face it, lying is nowhere near as bad as that. Especially since so few of that shower go to the gym.

Of course, the government – being made up of Irish people – has plenty to give out about and not take action on.

Things that shower wish would disappear and stop annoying them	Things that shower only loves
✳ Women.	✳ Cosying up to the Church.
✳ People who are differently abled.	✳ Not rocking boats.
✳ Low-income families.	✳ Partying (even at work!).
✳ Migrants, even refugees.	✳ Writing erotic novels.

* Greece.

* Women.

* Teachers.

* Anyone their da didn't introduce them to.

* Women.

* Wearing ear-plugs to drown out the giving out.

* Pinstripe suits.

* Big chunky necklaces.

* Leaving the back way.

* Unless there's a photo op.

So, vote however you like in the next general election and moan your face off about it before, during and after, as is our way. It'll make shag-all difference. But maybe you'll make yourself feel better.

Moan factor: 11/10

★

Tom in his cab:

'I'd that fella in me car during the last election campaign. TD fella. You know the one. Big red face on him, always laughing. Sure, they've loads to be laughing about. So I'm driving him home to his place – beautiful house, now, I have to say – but when we get there, "Turn back," says he.

'"Turn back where?" says I. "Amn't I after getting you home?"

'"I know yeah," says he, "but I need a slash."

'There's me wondering if there's something wrong with his own jacks and him with plenty money for a plumber. But then he tells me to drive to a spot not far away, so I do, and he gets out.

'I'm not looking, now, but in the rear-view out the corner of my eye, I see an election poster for one of the other shower, and it hanging low on a railing. You know, one of the ones with a young fella's big head with really white teeth staring out at you. Sure enough, yer man drops the cacks, and – he must have been burstin' now – he wees all over the poster! I could hear it from inside the cab – like a downpour it was! He was going for ages. Powerful is right.

'After a few minutes, he gets back in and I say nothing, but he's looking even more pleased with himself. "Home, James," says he, "and say nothing."

'"Right you are, your lordship," says I. Lovely fella, he was. A gentleman.'

Drips

★ Speaking of right showers . . . ★

Gentle rains, and rolling mists, the base ingredient for Guinness, the thing that separated us from oppressors and annoying tourists – we used to love water. Even the odd time we had to use our couches for rafts, at least it was free. Or so we naively thought. How could we have been so stupid, when we're well aware that the whole government is a *liar like the other shower*? Of course someone was going to find a way to charge us by the droplet.

But we could never have predicted the downright silliness that would be brought to us by Irish Water. Not the bottles of Irish water that come with added mists and myths and magical thirst-quenching properties: we've been happily paying for that since Celtic Tiger times. Back then, people would only brush their teeth in water with a backstory. No, Irish Water is . . . well, we've never really seen anything like it before.

We're not thick: we know we can't have clean water delivered to our homes without somehow paying to maintain pipes and fix leaks. We don't imagine water elves come with buckets in the night, filling our cisterns out of the goodness of their hearts. But Irish Water are almost as away with the fairies as those elves.

What Irish Water can't seem to agree on:

* How much a droplet should cost – about €1 million, probably.

* How to measure the droplets – we'll have to pay for a diviner to come to every home and sense our usage.

* Whether the droplets and the pipes they come in through are made of lead or not.

* What our names are and where we live. We all know each other. Getting our details wrong is impossible. Somehow, they managed it.

* Why they need our PPS numbers and dental records and fingerprints and menstrual cycles and what we dreamed about last night.

* Whether we should (a) pay for droplets in advance by guesstimating how thirsty or dirty we'll get over the course of a year or (b) whether we should save all our used droplets and show them to them at year's end, for proof.

* If (b), where we're supposed to store all the anti-evaporation vats.

* Whether we've already been paying for droplets via other taxes and charges ('You have, you haven't, you have, you haven't, you haven't, you haven't'…and so on).

Those elves are starting to look more realistic and reasonable by the second.

Then gleaming, shiny, expensive ads, with gleaming, shiny, expensive voices sounding distinctly, gleamingly, not confused, got everyone's backs well up. A lot of shouting ensued. It seemed like everyone was on the radio all the time but, on the upside, if you were stuck for an alias you could use whatever Irish Water had called you on the envelope. It would almost certainly not be your actual name.

Strangely, they brought the nation together. It takes a lot to get us on our feet. When austerity kicked in, we moaned: Greece took to the streets and Athens was on fire. It makes a certain sense that what finally brought us out in our thousands was the wet. It's our natural habitat. If we know anything, we know water.

You'd be dying for a cool glass of it after all that, wouldn't you? If only you could afford it.

Moan factor: 10/10

The Dhrop: Drugs and Drink

★ We'll just have the one ★

We love these. Oh, we love them. We beat everyone around the world at these. Blame genes, bad weather, unemployment and the state of the nation – plus, sadly, a tendency to depression: whatever you blame, we are the best at drugs and drink. (Or worst. Sure, we get it.)

This is another of those things we actively don't give out about enough, or give out about in the wrong way. We're a nation of addictive personalities and we congratulate each other on it. We're 'passionate'. We don't 'do things by halves' (see *Balance*). We have 'a real and pressing heroin problem'. But, you know, we can stop anytime. We just need a quick spliff before we write our next poem. Or a yoke before the next band comes on. It's because we're artists, really.

Everyone else on the planet knows that alcohol is a drug. Not us! We keep it in a separate box (or bottle) so no one can point the finger. *If my buddy's drinking at a socially acceptable level, then so am I.* Even if we're making daily deposits at the bottle bank. It's a great system.

So what's socially unacceptable drinking? Falling down? Check out your main street on a Saturday – they can't all be socially unacceptably drunk, can they? Surely that's just exuberance. Or having a rest near some vomit?

Or trying to break the world record for 'Most People doing 'Rock the Boat' outdoors'?

Some people feel that – like the sixties – if you remember a night, you weren't really there. Thankfully, most of the rest of the world got over the sixties – even Irish people wear sunscreen now and allow women to work. And cocaine seems to have fallen out of favour because having your heart stop is just so 1980s. But still we drink.

Drinking and driving? While most people with any bit of cop-on won't even think about it, this still went on far longer in Ireland than it should have. Because people gave out that they had to have their pint and sometimes the local wasn't quite local enough. In rural areas, you had to drive. How to get home? Those Irish Water elves aren't going to organise carriages at midnight. You can almost understand certain rural TDs campaigning against the drink-drive limit. Almost.

Hangovers are badges of honour ('You legend!'), and if you abstain, it's assumed you're pregnant or ill. When we do give out yards about drink, it's usually about how much it costs (see *Price of a Pint*).

Giving out that we don't have a problem doesn't help either, you ostrich-necked chancers. We patently do. The *Punch* cartoon drunken Irishman – though unfair – must have come from somewhere: the Italians or French in the strips were far less inebriated. We must have done something to suggest it. And, judging from our monkey-like appearance in those cartoons, we were overdue a wax, too.

Back to the 'artist' argument: one of the problems that stops us giving out is how very much we romanticise inebriation. It can seem as if our greatest writers, artists and poets were addicted to the drop and they were *cool*. So cool. We want us a piece of that action, and have our faces on souvenir tea towels alongside donkeys and pints. *You too can be James Joyce or Paddy Kavanagh! Sure we're all at the writing here. Buy me a pint and I'll tell you about it.*

Accident and Emergency might as well be a cool nightclub: at the weekend, sooner or later, you'll see everyone you know. Wouldn't it be even cooler to see A&E waiting times decimated, minus alcohol-related injuries? But then we'd lose overcrowding to give out about. We never said this would make sense.

And let's not forget, in this country, alcohol brings in a lot of money, so JOBS.

Ciarán:

'When manufacturers say, "Drink responsibly", do they mean "Don't spill"? Cos, like, that's a real challenge.'

Even Ciarán knows they're not suggesting drinking less of the product they've just made a massive shiny ad in America for.

It's yummy and fun. But could we maybe agree to give out a little more about alcohol? Sorrows don't really drown, you know. Those feckers can swim.

Moan factor: 7.5% proof/10

E is for ...

Emigr8ion Gener8ion

★ Better out than in ★

It's ba-ack! You thought it was gone – and it was, for a while, during the Celtic Tiger – but emigration is right back on the giving-out table. It's for every generation. That's why we've given it a little spelling update in the heading, to appeal to the SMS gener8ion it now affects. Hardly anyone is staying any more. Tourists are staying longer than citizens, and they're only here for about two weeks.

It's just like the eighties, nostalgia fans! When we all learned French because the only place we'd have a chance of a job was Brussels, or tutoring others so *they* could go to Brussels. The recurring topics in oral exams were unemployment, emigration and AIDS, just in case we'd forgotten how crap everything would be after we left school. Oh, we might have looked as if all we cared about was back-combing and leg-warmers, but we had a lot on our minds.

And it looks like little has changed. We've slotted right back into an Irish tradition dating from Famine times: getting out. To Britain, we went, or America. Travel conditions were cramped and terrible, whether you're talking coffin ships or Ryanair. But chancing either was better than staying.

They say those of us who did stay were the runts: physically weak and a bit thick. Feck off! If you survived all the crap going on here, through Independence, Civil War, Dev and ABJCMcQ's The Shushening, you're actually looking at some pretty tough cookies. We gave out yards, we coped, we did our best to enjoy it.

But here we are, leaving again. It's only a matter of time till the next round of emigration songs starts rolling in.

When you do come back (you will), just make sure you use what you've learned abroad to give out yards about how shite Ireland is compared to where you were. Welcome home.

Moan factor: 9/10

Golden rules for an emigration song:

* ✳ Have a short memory. You must have forgotten – even forgiven – Ireland's woes. Sing only its praises.

* ✳ It should be in English, so the people in your Philadelphia flat-share can understand it.

- Sing about how much you miss the greenness and bogs you only visited once on a school tour.

- Sing about stealing corn, even though you thought it came in a can.

- Something about Trevelyan. ('The Fields of Athenry' is probably the apex of the genre. See *Soccer*.)

- But sing up, sing on. We miss you, too.

Ciarán replying to a post on emigration on a forum called Whinelist:

Dude, go all you like. It's fine. All the more jobz 4 us. I don't have one yet but I contribute loads to the pizza sector. I'm delighted 4 u that you enjoy Belgium but if you had any balls, you'd have gone to America like you really wanted. I've never been, but I've played a lot of games set there. Going to Europe (or as I call it, Bigger Ireland) is a copout and you know it. If you're going to leave, leave properly – somewhere where you couldn't technically walk or swim home. Soz, but ur pathetic.

★

Eurovision: The Great War

★ Here are the results from the Irish jury ★

You'd hardly think a shiny excuse for European broadcasters to showcase local tourist sights and home-grown choreographers would raise hackles in Ireland, but of course it does.

There was a time when we used to win this all the time. *All* the time. It brought great unity as we gathered around our TV sets in our Johnny Logan scarves. Those were the days when we could have sent a castanet-playing donkey and still got *douze points* across the board. Uncharacteristically for us, we got complacent about winning. We never win anything. Great for giving out; awful for our collective self-esteem.

But we were great at Eurovision. We might have disappeared early from Wimbledon or the Olympics, but we were the best at writing songs and singing songs and wearing big dresses or tinfoil space suits, while singing songs. Other countries agreed and went on telly to say so.

Oh, the sweet, sweet validation!

The king of all the half-time shows ever was, of course, *Riverdance*; we're still milking that one. We give out about all the other half-time shows. 'Fireworks? Not enough hard-shoe work.' 'A full-blown ballet on ice? Where's Flatley?' 'Was that half of Cirque du Soleil? Would've been better with a hooded choir.' We really aren't going to let this one go.

The voting politics give everyone plenty to gripe about. Now text votes let Eurovision fans at home decide, the Eastern Europeans – almost as if they hadn't ever heard of Ireland or Johnny Logan *at all*! – all but ignored us. They didn't seem to know that you're supposed to give us *douze points* if we've bothered to enter, even if we've entered Jedward (so to speak).

If you win, you get to host it, which is a really expensive prize. We can't even afford to stabilise the sets of our TV dramas, so how could we possibly be expected to stump up for disco balls and glitter guns? Luckily, hosting it hasn't been a problem in a while. Great song, Sweden. Great song.

If we had to host the Eurovision now, we'd have to hold it in the news studio, with the RTÉ Symphony Orchestra – conducted by the immortal soul of Noel Kelehan – playing out in the hall. You could say that, in a way, by ignoring us, the eastern bloc is doing us a kindness.

Moan factor: *Nul points*/10

mEejits

★ Meeja Eejits ★

The way some people give out about the media, you'd swear everyone involved was an eejit or a liar, and not the good kind either. It's often pronounced *meeja* as if all meeja eejits – mEejits – have an accent from Dublin 4 and so are a bit up themselves because they live near RTÉ (pr. *OR-teeyee*) and some embassies.

Dismissing the entire media as run by eejits is great because you can then give out yards about them non-stop. The ultimate in hypocrisy, you'll usually be using the media or someone in it to get your giving-out point across. You don't have to have an objective point of view – you certainly don't believe they do – and it's a great focus and outlet for our tendency to paranoia and suspicion. Well done, mEejits!

Moan factor: 7.5/10

Common accusations of meejitry:

* They're all against me. I never hear anyone I agree with on air.

* They've been hypnotised or paid off by old-school villains or REDACTED.

* I and my kind are being silenced because reasons.

* I'm sure that producer/editor is a part-time bishop.

* Oh, sure they all know each other. Their backs

are sore from the slapping. I don't know where they find the time to keep up with current affairs with all the massaging.

* You'd think #marian & #miriam were the only women with mic access.

* Everyone who works at that paper is a kind of a spy.

* Yer man is married to yer woman – of course he'd say that. It's not what he thinks, though.

* They'd never have said that if they hadn't seen it on Twitter.

Eggs

★ Giving out over easy ★

By now you may be suffering a sort of moan-hangover. We have one word for you. Eggs!

Yes, even breakfast can provide an opportunity to give out – some would say the most important giving out of the day. Eggs can deliver a decent old morning moan before you've even had your second cup of tea.

★

How You Like Them Done	Fried
✳ Whether or not cooked breakfasts are bad for you.	✳ So what? You want a fry.
✳ Whether you'd prefer an omelette or a frittata at the brunch place.	✳ Is no one listening? You said fried.
✳ Boiled eggs are never done right. Whether you're a busy executive with only three minutes for cooking or you're at home at your ma's, no one in Ireland has ever cooked boiled eggs right. (It may be the association with soldiers.)	✳ Exactly. So fry 'em.

Fried eggs cure hangovers and boiled eggs (yes, even those tricky feckers) have been known to clear up the flu, even though that's not possible. The Irish endow eggs with almost magical properties. But we'll still give out about them.

If you're talking ovaries, well, actually, don't. Even the mention of them can lead you down a rabbit hole you're probably not able for when you were only after a chat. We'll explore this later in *Vagina Owners*. For now, just keep your egg talk shelly.

Moan factor: 2/10

Ciarán reviews *Eggsactly*, a new brunch place, on BrunchReviews.com:

I'm never normally up on Sundays, but Eggsactly sounded like it didn't suck too much. Plus it's really near my house. And first impressions were good. I dug the egg motif – shell-shaped chairs with yolk yellow cushions and plates shaped like fried eggs. So, eggs, I got it.

But then I got over it. I was asked to queue and I hate that. I was offered a table outside if I wanted it. I did NOT. I burn super-easily.

Unlike the food here . . . When I finally got seated (luckily I had two Batman comics to read or I'd have been outtathere) it was all 'delicately' this and 'lightly' that, which is some BULLSHIT. Sunday breakfast is meant to be nuked, man. Like, it's got to be crisp and Star Wars-level chewy, otherwise there's no point leaving the house. Even for a great Wookiee reference.

And what the absolute what is brioche when it's at home? It's like bread that wants to be cake but can't be arsed. I was given it for free when I didn't like my 'eggs floating near a gentle shore of chilled-out bacon, nestling in a cocoon of hash-brown heaven under a mushroom-foam cloudy sky' but I almost paid them to take it back again.

The waitress girl was nice, but I couldn't in all conscience leave a tip after all that. Brunch is just an excuse to pretend breakfast has happened, when really it's just an insulting lunch preview. Never again.

Star rating: 1 out of 5 eggs (and that's for the chairs)

F is for . . .

Finances

★ Trust funds? ★

We don't like this word any more. We didn't before, but we hate it now. This goes way beyond giving out: it's practically mourning.

MONEY WORDS THAT MAKE IRISH PEOPLE'S
BUTTS CLENCH

✳ Austerity (don't say it! You'll summon it!) .	✳ Debt.
✳ Bailout.	✳ Finance.
✳ Banker.	✳ Financial adviser.
✳ Bonus.	✳ Fiscal (shudder).
✳ Certain Shifty Family Names.	✳ Mortgage.
✳ Charges.	✳ Rate.

On hearing these words, we scream. We cry. We shout at the TV, the radio or the street.

People who use this kind of language got us; they got us good. They hypnotised us with fake good fortune, then took all our stuff. We were told only eejits wouldn't get on the property ladder (see *Rung Up*). Nobody wants to be an eejit. So everyone got on the ladder. There isn't a lot of room on a ladder. We soon fell over. And then they kicked us in the eye.

We're wise to banks now and the finance fellas won't fool us again. Oh, no. Not till our next fake bit of good fortune, anyway. That said, it looks like the chancers have only gone and made a comeback. Why don't we lay ourselves down in front of their swishy new 'financial' 'advice' 'clinics', right now? They're going to end up wiping their feet on us anyway. We may as well cut to the chase.

Moan factor: Billions in debt/10

Fun

★ We really can give out about anything ★

We love fun. We're renowned for it. We couldn't give out about this, surely? Ah, we can!

The only circumstances under which Irish people are traditionally allowed to have fun:

* In defiance of some kind of hardship or adversity.

* If you feel guilty about it for ages till you forget you had fun in the first place.

＊ The word 'craic' was invented as a way to talk about having fun while not saying 'fun' and revealing how much of it you were having, or planning to have.

We hate it when someone else is having more fun than we are and we'll soon cut them down to size. 'They've lost the run of themselves,' we'll say, eyeing the people on the chair-o-planes with the deepest of suspicion. It'd never dawn on us to buy ourselves a ticket and get in the queue.

Moan factor: 2/10

We asked our experts what they do for fun:

Seán: Walking the fields with Betty after mass on Sunday. Dinner on at home. Lovely.

Ciarán: Annihilating someone's character in a comments section. That is hawt.

Tom: Fun? I'm freelance. I work for myself. I don't get to have fun. I get no time off. Fun? The state of you.

Máiréad: I suppose I feel the most satisfaction when I get a great deal on an oven glove on eBay. But life is full of suffering. I try never to forget that.

Scamall: I spin. Not on a bike or a wheel, just me. Preferably outside, on the spot. I just stick my arms out and I spin and I spin and I spin.

Pity the Fools

★ Sometimes you're paranoid, sometimes you're right ★

It's our judgemental, always-slightly-suspicious edge that makes us such good givers-out. We're always ready with the bitter word. Sometimes, though, it's justified. We don't suffer fools gladly. Like a nation of Mr. Ts, we pity them.

There's barely a more cutting remark in Hiberno-English than 'That fella's a right fool'. Or just 'Fool'. Simple, swear-free, effective. If you ever hear this said about you, it's time to up your game or you'll be talked about behind your back. And no need to ask what they're saying. We'll tell you right now – what they'll be saying is: 'Fool.'

Hurts, doesn't it?

Moan factor: 3/10

F-Bombs

★ You know they're not really bombs? ★

You know that outrage when a live radio guest accidentally swears? They apologise immediately (if they even realise). Everyone in the studio laughs. But then the switchboard gets jammed and there are at least fifty letters to the paper?

No, you're right. That doesn't happen. Nobody is offended any more, not really. There might be one Miffed in Mullingar and maybe a Shocked in Sligo, but if we're honest we don't care. We've plenty else to be giving out about and, besides, we're well used to it. Everyone curses here, even small babies.

Some of our first words are swears – in fact, swears should probably be our third official language after Irish and English. Swear words on our passport would be an accurate reflection of life here. The sign at airport Arrivals should read *Fáilte the F Romhat*. They could put it right beside the *Drive on the Left / Conduire à Gauche* signs, to let you know what to really expect from your visit.

There's nothing wrong with a good old swear: it purges ill feeling, vents spleen, spices up a sentence and adds rhythm where we feel the need for punch. We don't feel certain sentences are fully finished without it. We even made up 'feck' so we could swear without really swearing.

Swearing's like poetry when we do it, or so we hear. Your nan does it and so do you. If we weren't such cute hoors, we'd admit to being proud of it. And why not? We'll never be great skiers.

If there were a Eurovision Swears Contest, I'm telling you now we would still be winning it. Máiréad would picket such a contest, and that's exactly why Scamall submitted this as an entry.

Eurovision Swear Song

Look at my big f****** shoulder-pads
They're such a f****** beautiful sight
My love suit is shiny, I may look like a p****
But I'm so in love I couldn't give a sh***
(Chorus)
Let me be your love lang*r, love lang*r, love
This isn't pretending
It's not a love stunt
Let me be your love lang*r, love lang*r, love
But if you don't, I won't call you a c***.

(Scamall felt conflicted about the last word: she never normally uses it as a derogatory term. But she knew it would annoy Máiréad. And that Máiréad would realise which word it was, even when they bleeped it out on *The Late Late Show*. It came second in the National Song Contest. Who can say what it could have done in Europe?)

So, know that if someone inadvertently swears on the radio and A.N. Other leaps on that F-bomber, A.N. Other is a bit of a hypocrite – but when have the Irish ever let hypocrisy get in the way of a good old rant?

Máiréad to her local radio station:

'Oh, I've never been so insulted. That kind of language has no place on the airwaves or anywhere near my ears.'
(Translation: 'Oh, I'm having to hold in some beautiful swears of my own right now – some I made up myself – and they're straining to spring forth from my mouth like they normally do when there's no one else around.')
Máiréad: 'It's rude and disrespectful and it's everywhere now. I blame the internet: I never even heard a swear before 1995.'
(Translation: 'I miss being able to use the discriminatory swears I used to be able to use before people on Twitter told me I couldn't.')

Of course, it's nice to have manners. Don't shoehorn in a coarse word where a non-expletive will do. Try not to swear when getting a medal from the president, for instance, or conducting a baptism.

But if you're Irish, you love to swear. People only give out about this when they're really, really bored.

Luckily, we almost always have something else to give out about. And thank fuck for that.

Moan factor: F/10

Fluoriding the Waves

★ There must be something in the water ★

We only used to hear about this in toothpaste ads. Now it seems to take up about 50 per cent of the airwaves and print media.

We're not scientists but, then, neither are most fluoride-haters. According to them, fluoride in the water is the end of the world, an inlet for alien mind-control. Or something. And there we thought it had just been controlling our dental caries. Scary.

Scamall campaigns against water fluoridation (of course she does), even though she's mad about her teeth and has never had a sick day in her life despite drinking fluoridated water for over fifty years. There's a fair whack of it in the fancy bottled water she buys when she wants to look sophisticated, too. But never mind that.

Moan factor: I'm not a dentist/10

Scamall writes to her local council:

Brian
I'm writing to you again, because you seem to have lost my last few letters. I know my home-made recycled mulch paper disintegrates if not handled with due care and respect for its origins, but this is ridiculous.

Even though I've seen no change in my own health, I'm hearing a lot of stuff about fluoride in the media and I'm getting very worried. I can't see a toothpaste ad now without having to use an inhaler. And I hate conventional medicine, as you know, so this is really heavy.

It's bad enough to have concerned citizens' allegations about fluoride shot down by scientists and medics, but now we're being ignored by our own council. This really is proof, if proof were needed, of a big conspiracy to pump fluoride into us for some reason. Why not buy a fluoride gun, while you're at it, and shoot it at us while we're walking around? It's the same!

From what I saw in one magazine, a build-up of fluoride over time does something. I'm not sure what but I don't want to wait around to find out.

Please get back to me. Please read my earlier letters. If you can't find them, just follow the smell.

Yours, in furious hope,

Scamall de Spéir

Food! Food! Food?

★ Biting the hands that feed us ★

Food blogging has really taken off in Ireland recently. We only heard of cappuccinos a hot minute ago and we're still not comfortable with kale being a superfood (it's a side dish to bacon, people), so you'll forgive us if this is a bit hard to digest.

Ireland's now thriving in terms of food and cooking, so of course people have a right to say what they think. They're paying good money. But being able to give out instantly and publicly about eating has made us all giving-out gourmands. It's not clear how we all became experts: ten years ago we wouldn't have known a foam or a *jus* if they'd come up and bitten us. Now it seems everyone has a caramelising blow-torch under their sink. And a food critique* to share.

After his brunch-adventure-slash-brioche-disaster, Ciarán got a taste for food blogs. However, he now only deals with his staple food, the takeaway:

I did not think you could get pizza wrong. It is, after all, pizza. But a local pizzeria (which shall remain nameless as I still have to use them) almost ruined my life the other night.

As you know, if you read this blog regularly (hi, guys), pizza is kind of like a god to me.

---

* Fancy way of saying 'giving out about grub'.

I would totally marry a pizza if they would have a referendum for that. But, seeing as they probably won't, I'll have to stay single for a while and keep ordering in.

Guys, these douches delivered a pizza without cheese. I mean, WTAF? That's not 'pizza' – that's a hot flat sandwich with anchovies, and no one eats anchovies. No one. They would die. By the time I realised their disgusting mistake, the pizza dude was long gone and it was too late to do anything about it. No way was I calling them to complain, because what good would that do? I was hungry now.

So, I tried it. I was forced to try the WTAF no-cheese gross-anchovy 'pizza' and you know what? It didn't suck. I mean, it sucked a little bit because my mouth was all, like, ready for cheese. But I didn't die – shock – and it did taste kind of like pizza. A lot like anchovies, but also like pizza.

To sum up, sometimes a surprise can be okay. I wouldn't do it again, though.

See you at the door.

Key-ron

★

G is for . . .

Godsapalooza

★ Shaking our fists at the heavens ★

We won't go into the Big Guy too much here: (a) it's been done and (b) lots of people think He's cool, and that's fine.

Instead, let's have a look at who or what we worshipped before St Patrick brought his bushels of shame to this country, ushering in The Shushening. The Shushening Ushering. There were loads of gods to choose from. Did we give out about them? Answer: DUH. Of course we did.

MADE-UP FACT

St Patrick and the Bushels of Shame was an ancient band that played the ancient Shushening Ushering Music Festival. We know this because there's an ancient programme with the line-up written on an ancient ogham stone in Meath.

Before St Pat brought Christianity, it was godsapalooza all up in this place. We were guilt-free pagans with a god for everything. Goddesses, too – imagine. Life was hard and the weather was as bad as ever, but these were good times – with so many deities to choose from, you were never lonely. And if you gave out about one, you could always shift focus to another. If you felt Brighid hadn't helped you out with your blacksmithing, for instance, you could call on Lugh for some trickery or multi-tasking. It would have been hard to stay mad at the whole of the Tuatha Dé Danann, for gods' sake! It'd be like trying to be mad with the whole cast of *Friends*: there's always one you like. And, like *Friends*, gods are everywhere, all the time.

So while gods would have been given out about, there was always another one to pick up the slack or help you out with your crops. It was a fine arrangement.

But then along came what's-his-crozier. (That's Patrick. Keep up.) He told the pagans – us – that there was only One Big Lad and, with a wave of his magic shamrock, he did away with all the other lads and lassies we'd known and worshipped. In place of practically daily festivals we were now only allowed Christmas, Easter and a week-long festival of alcohol and green face-paint named after himself. (Patrick's Day. Still with us?) Guilt and shame were doled out by the bushel and here we are today.

If only the God of Giving Out had stepped in. If she had, The Shushening might never have happened.

Moan factor: 3/10

Scamall calls *Livewhine* to talk religion:

'I'm the kind of person who doesn't believe in God, Jer. I mean, I'm spiritual – I'm Cancerian, so of course

I am. But I don't see why rules make someone any better than the other. If you think belonging to an organised religion makes you superior, then you've never tried to catch a goat on a rainy sacrifice day. If you still believe what you believe after that, then you really know what faith is.'

MADE-UP FACT

'Faith' is the name of most sacrificial nanny goats. Billygoats are just called 'Bill'.

The Gays

★ We will survive (The Shushening) ★

With the passing of the Marriage Equality Referendum, 2015 was a landmark year for the LGBT community in Ireland. But the run-up was very shouty. There was a heck of a lot of giving out and shouting and talking over people. It seemed some people were shocked, because the LGBT community is brand new here.

Kidding!

It's as old as the Tuatha Dé Danann themselves. In fact, accounts of Ireland long ago seem to suggest we were totally cool with whoever you were and whoever you wanted to bump uglies with. You think Cúchulainn and Ferdia were 'just good friends' with amazing abs? Liked a bit of a cuddle after a shower, that kind of thing? Listen, people simply don't write epic poems about or carve statues of 'just good friends' no matter how impressive their daytime warrioring. Or their abs.

Post-St Patrick and his bushels of shame (still a great band name), during The Shushening we all had to hide our sexuality. Cover it, in a big cloak. Especially if the kind of sex we preferred didn't automatically lead to reproduction – which, according to Pat and his friends Dev and ABJCMcQ, was Ireland's brand-new job and goal in life.

Sex was now a shame-filled duty. You were definitely not to have sex for pleasure or intimacy. Definitely, *definitely* not with someone of the same sex: sure, how could you have babies, then – the only reason to have sex in the first place, the three to five times in your life that you have it? So, historically, there's been a lot of giving out about The Gays.

In the heads of people obsessed with the idea, anything but straight sex seems to be some kind of wild, raw, animal affair. The idea of this amount of craic wrecks the heads of the Shusheners, even though they made it up in those same heads. This leads to overuse of the word 'sperm' in televised debates. They just can't seem to get sperm out of their heads. But, to be honest, it spices up dull debates for the rest of us.

Then, in 2015, it seems Ireland got tired of the shame-cloak. Something stirred in our ancient pagan loins, reminded us who we really were and got us to the polls to vote Yes to love. At the end of the day, we all want the same things. Love. Security. Family. A better, more modern Ireland. Great dance music. Great abs.

The campaign battle was bloody and dirty but hopefully, now, Cúchulainn and Ferdia can be proud of us. Shame-cloaks are so last year.

> Máiréad wrote a poem about this. She's mulling whether to put it to music and maybe enter it into the Eurovision, as a response to Scamall's sweary one.

You can keep your sperm in Denmark
We've enough here of our own
Please keep your sperm in Denmark
Well inside your Eurozone
We don't want your seed donations
From some kind of Viking bank
It's all I can seem to think about
I can't even have a . . . tank
To think in.

The end doesn't scan very well, but a good arranger will get the backing singers to do it.

Moan factor: 10/10

Ghostclusters

★ Who you gonna call? Jer, of course ★

We don't have the official figures, but we almost definitely have more ghosts per capita in Ireland than we have golf courses, and that's a hell of a lot (see *Tee Party*). We know this because people call Jer to give out about them – and not all of them B&B owners who could use the lucrative ghost-hunter bookings. Ghosts seem to haunt castles, old forts and Glasnevin cemetery, pubs, clubs and B&Bs that don't have great views, or vicinity to a national monument.

We have a special relationship with ghosts. We're a superstitious lot. And vain. We secretly believe we're such good craic that no one could possibly want to leave us for eternity. So they stick around. Whole political parties have been known to refuse to die, stumbling around the mortal world for years and years past their sell-by date. Chilling.

Some people give out that there's no such thing as ghosts – almost as if they didn't want the tourists to come. And some give out that they can't get rid of their father-in-law, long after he's passed on. But if you want to get rid of a ghost, just make sure to talk to Jer and the entire country. Believe us, everyone will have an opinion on whether you need a priest or a ghostbuster.

Moan factor: Boo/10

Tom in his cab:

'I'd a ghost in the cab once. You don't believe me? Oh, I did, now. Shockin' quiet fella he was. It was Hallowe'en night and everyone else was hoppin' off the walls, so 'twas his quietness gave him away. I asked him a few questions, being polite. 'Boo,' says he. Well, I didn't question him further, let me put it that way. He was all dressed in grey, fierce pale and floating about an inch off the seat . . . I could see him in the rear-view mirror. No seat belt, either, but I suppose he was already . . . y'know . . . Anyway, he was going to Dublin Castle, and when I pulled up on Dame Street he got out. "Do ghosts carry euros?" says I, hintin'. Kind of messin' but no way was I letting anyone off without paying, alive or dead. "Boo," says he again, and off he goes, in through the gates. Now, when I say "through the gates" I mean "through the gates". The stone part. The pillar, like. I wasn't one bit impressed. Stiffed by a stiff. Who'd have thought? Feckin' Hallowe'en.'

★

Getting Around

★ Giving out about travel ★

Getting around locally

(Or giving out about the buses)

Loads to give out about here:

* The state of the buses. The *state* of them.

* You'd miss the conductors all the same.

* The heating's never on.

* It's too hot.

* The replacement driver never came and you sat on the bus till the original driver's next shift.

* The prices have gone up too much.

* The real-time app has said '*Ann*' ('Due') for twenty-seven minutes now, with no sign of a bus. Either it's wrong, or the bus has been sucked into some kind of vortex. That's very worrying.

* You're taking your life in your hands on a night-bus.

* You had to stand the length of the route of the 39A.

Or, if you want to give out about giving out about the buses:

* They're the best way to get around for the price.

* They have the Wi-Fi now, you know.

* There's nothing you can't see from the top deck.

* Old folks travel free and they're always up for a chat.

* A driver took you an extra few stops for free to make sure you got home safe.

The buses are almost as useful for giving out in Ireland as the weather is. (See *Weather*.)

When bus drivers go on strike, the country comes to a standstill. Busy towns go all post-zombie-apocalypse. So it's clear they're the backbone of getting around here and we're always relieved and happy when they come rumbling back to our roads. We still love to give out about them, though.

'The buses' as a topic will keep you going for ages. Unlike – if givers-out are to be believed – the buses themselves.

The next Getting Around level takes us farther afield.

Getting around the island 1
(Getting from town to town. Or more buses)

Everyone has boarded a coach on a rainy Friday from Busáras to wherever you're from. It's a rite of passage.

Nowadays, coach travel is really nothing to give out about. There are a million companies, amazing motorways (short, but still), Wi-Fi . . . Today's coach users don't know they're born.

Time was when you had to snake slowly out of cities, stopping in every town and village ever, with at least one breakdown and the replacement bus at least two hours away. Even if that didn't happen, and it wasn't raining, you still had to stop in Urlingford or Kinnegad because RULES. Bus drivers only did half the route, swapped buses and went back the way they'd come. Even they couldn't hack the whole journey – and they were getting paid for it. As soon as you unfurled your pretzel body from the back of the bus, you gave out. If you still had the strength.

Getting around the island 2
(Trains)

See 'Getting around locally'. It's really much the same but better now than it used to be. And, helpfully, we've invented Roboconductors™ (See *Roboconductors™*), so the bit that wasn't sorted is now sorted. Sorted.

Getting off the island
(Overseas travel)

If you live in Ireland, you will have had to do this kind of travel at some stage. You may never have done a Grand Tour of Europe, like a Victorian gent, or been an eighties Interrailer, but you've definitely had to go somewhere off our shores. No one born on an island really believes in the rest of the world until they've seen it.

Luckily, we no longer have to risk our lives crossing the Atlantic on coffin ships, but there's still plenty for us to moan about whenever we do take a trip. Off. The Island.

Actually, there is a small proportion of Irish people who never do leave, unless there's a wedding. These are probably the ones who give out the most about travel. They are 'not good travellers'. They would have been the worst people to kidnap had you been a pirate in the seventeenth century: you'd have had to shove them off at the next port or fed them to the sharks, no matter how much you'd originally hoped you'd get for them in a Tunisian slave market.

Couple of things about Irish people abroad. As much as we give out about tourists, we're no saints or scholars ourselves. We've all watched from behind half-parted fingers as a revved-up group of compatriots shouts, 'Amhrán na bhFiann' at each other in a Chicago nightclub, or caught a flash of green shorts when you've just been mooned in Torremolinos.

But, when giving out about travel, are these lads and lassies our target? Not really. It's the lads and lassies themselves who give out about 'abroad'.

For example:

* There's nowhere to watch the GAA match.

* Nowhere serves 'Irish food' (whatever that is. Crisps?).

* People abroad are 'no craic'. (Translation: the Australian authorities simply wouldn't put up with our shit and sent us home.)

If you've ever taken a flight between Dublin and London at six a.m., you'll see the reason behind another travel give-out: because we travel so often, we've become travel experts and now we pity the fools who aren't.

Sharp-suited Irish men and women (carrying briefcases that, of course, fit neatly in the overhead compartment) fly over and back for meetings, without taking in a single sight, barely pausing to hydrate. This is their regular commute: they get rightly annoyed when others faff.

We became experts at airport security during the seventies and eighties during a quite different aspect of The Shushening: we were supposedly the terrorists *du jour*. All of us – even your nan. We still can't believe it if we don't get searched. 'What? Did I get an upgrade? Is it my birthday?' So, we know.

Here's a handy guide to how not to be a pitied fool when at security with Irish people.

~~~~~~

A guide to not pissing irish people off and having them give out about you at the airport:

* Take off your overcoat, shoes, belt, etc., BEFORE you approach the conveyor belt. YES, every time. If we can do it twenty meters out, twenty minutes before our first caffeine fix of the day, you can too.

* Same goes for your laptop. Unsheath that bad boy. YES, every time.

* Remember, only little teeny-tiny bottles of shampoo and other liquids are allowed. This adorable-fluids-only policy has been in place since 2002. This can't be news to you.

* If you dither you will be tutted at. Repeatedly. You could cut the tension in the airport air with a knife. But you won't get that big knife past security. What made you think you could bring a big knife?

* No self-respecting Irish frequent flyer ever wraps gifts: they used to end up in controlled explosions – no matter whose birthday it was.

> You can't be waiting around for that when you've a meeting in London at ten a.m.

✳ We don't make jokes about having bombs in our bags or explosive personalities.

✳ Ironically, our 'tut' reflex could take down a light aircraft. But keep that quiet till at least the Duty Free.

Note re. Ryanair: Relationship status: still complicated. Too many times they've made us beg for something we thought we'd already paid for and then made us *pay extra* for it at Stansted. But their recent marketing strategy has been interesting. They seem to have been instructing staff to treat passengers like . . . What is it again? *Humans?* It's weird and unfamiliar. It's fun watching them do the begging for a change, but sometimes you'd almost miss the whole being-transported-like-cargo experience.

Moan factor: 5/10

Gullnado
★ When seabirds attack ★

In terms of sheer seaside terror (and ubiquity), *Sharknado* has nothing on the current attack being perpetrated on the country by seagulls. To listen to some commentators, even *Jaws* was less of a threat, and he took a bite out of a boat.

In the summer of 2015, it seemed that seagulls were in the national news almost daily. Everyone was giving out about them. They were behind everything from casual chip theft to sheep rustling, not to mention a lot of white shite. They stole ice-creams from innocent children and terrorised small dogs. As such, they were deemed 'a threat to society' and there was a call for a cull. A cull-call. A gull-cull-call.

Against this were the conservationists saying gulls were endangered, driven inland (and thus to crime) by our own overfishing of their staples and lured by the smell of the luscious litter we leave behind in most places we go. We don't give out about that. We don't have to. It's somehow the gulls' fault.

Anyway, you've been warned. Don't leave your chips unguarded on the pier or your drink unguarded in a nightclub: a gull might sidle up, slip you something – and then take your chips.

Moan factor: 9.9/10

★

ℋ is for . . .

Hedge-Hogging

★ Giving out knows no bounds ★

Ah, the humble hedgerow. Lush, green, oxygenating our air. Marking the edge of the road. A habitat for little birds and mice. Nothing to give out about here, right?

Wrong.

Centuries ago, our natural coverage, the oak, was felled to make British ships and cathedral ceilings and the like. Now, we make do with less majestic coverage, like hedges. Nothing wrong with a hedge, it's just no oak. We've never really got over it. Hedges remind us of what we've lost.

Hedge schools were where Catholic children were taught long ago. The school might not always have been in an actual hedge, but let's just say that the AV equipment was probably not much to look at. Hedge schools taught spelling, multiplication and, presumably, hedge observation. But it wasn't all fun. It must have been rubbish if the rain could wash away your homework, or a dog really did eat it, because he was right there. In the hedge.

On top of that, we rely heavily on hedges as boundaries and, as we know, everyone gives out about those. We've been known to use hedges instead of employing a lawyer for 'demarcation of property bounds' (keeping the neighbours out). It's easy to go over a line if you're a hedge: hedges don't know about property law and it's not your fault if yours grew a little bit sideways and you had to widen the path, now is it?

On the other hand, it's pretty easy to erase a hedge if it might benefit you. Just ignore the cries of the fieldmice and tiny birds and rip it up. Burn it down. It's just a hedge, what's everyone crying about? You never even noticed that furze; you won't miss it when it's gone. But someone will. And there will be war.

More hedge beefs:

* Are they growing into the road? No wonder you cycled into the ditch.

* Should they be trimmed? If so, is this the council's responsibility? I'm not doing it. I hurt my hand when I cycled into the ditch.

* How much hedge is too much hedge? Or too little?

* What eejit turned this one into a heron? Have you too much time on your hands? And can I've my Strimmer back?

* Where's the hedge going on its holidays and would it like a manicure with that trim?

* Get off my land.

* That's a heritage hedge. You can't touch that.

You never knew hedges were so exciting, did you? See? High Drama everywhere. You just have to know where to look. (Clue: a hedge.)

So if your question was:'Can we find a reason to give out about naturally occurring foliage?' Of course we can.

Moan factor: 7/10

The Chronicle carried a story about a hedge-related court case in which Seán was involved.

A local man has been tried at the Circuit Court for impersonating a sheep when entering another man's land via his hedge. Trevor Lawless, a neighbour of Seán McCarthy of Topfield Farm, said there was an ancient right of way following the route of the hedge, and that it was a handy shortcut to his property from the road.

McCarthy gave evidence that Lawless had been told he had no right of way, and was to take the long way round as had been suggested before. Garda Mick Standin gave evidence that Lawless had been obstreperous and wool-covered on apprehension, and that McCarthy was generally a reasonable man.

McCarthy, he said, had no real objection to Lawless using the path, but 'it was the way he did it.' 'He knew straight away that he [Lawless] wasn't a sheep. Sheep don't wear cheap Italian shoes, or any kind of shoes for that matter. He took me [McCarthy] for a fool and no man should have to stand for that on his own land.'

The session was adjourned for lunch around the corner and sentence will be passed before tea time.

To be continued . . .

Hacked Off
★ Online secrets and lies ★

One night, after a little too much Smirnoff Ice, Ciarán (posting as Slyfox99) got a bit angry:

Slyfox99: U R ALL FASCISTS! I will bring U down. I cud totes bring down a govt so hacking U wud be NP.

Gingerfingers: Wot R U talking abt, man? U just asked me how to get a virus off ur system y'day 😀

Slyfox99: FASCIST! 😠

Seems like everyone everywhere is afraid of hackers and Ireland's no exception. We're a little in awe of their technological prowess and also secretly proud when we find out any of them are Irish. *Go on, lads! It was worth the taxpayers' money to put the computer lab into the school!*

Many of us – the government, for example – have things we'd prefer to keep hidden, and we live in deathly fear of a hacker deciding to nab our holiday snaps and stick them all over the internet.

Very few white Irish people take nude photos of themselves. Not out of prudery or the bushels of shame, but because we're just so very pale. We cause flare. It takes an entire camera crew a full day to make a white Irish person not flare. Believe me, there are no flattering non-flare selfies of a white Irish person in existence – not for want of trying, but there aren't. So, save your energy. But if a nude pic of a white Irish person were to get out there, it could take down the internet. That's right, the whole internet.

A Note On Irish Celebrity

Irish celebrities are possibly the only people in the world not afraid of being hacked. Every single image of them ever taken has already been released. We know their birthdays, their hopes and fears and what their downstairs loo looks like ('quirky/tasteful'), thanks to endless 'At Home With ...' articles and reveal-all shoots.

Ireland's so small, we either went to school with the celebrity in question ourselves or they're our second cousin and the whole family 'was always like that, going back'. Maybe it's because we already know so much that Irish celebrities want us to know even more. Or maybe they just really, really want photos of their downstairs loo to reach an even bigger audience. That's why they all end up on *Celebrity Big Brother* as the 'Irish hopeful'. That 'hope' has been thus redefined is a tragedy of our times.

Irish people handle celebrities by ignoring them. Not just pretending they don't recognise them – which would be 'giving him/her the satisfaction' – that's just the warm-up. We actually give them worse service than we would our regular customers. It helps to keep everyone in their place.

Then there's the more serious form of hacking. Whistle-blowers. There have been a few here recently who put the country's interests ahead of their own comfort and they managed to change things. They took a lot of flak, but we're grateful they did.

MADE-UP FACT

A new boyband called The Whistleblowers will be next year's *Celebrity Big Brother* Irish hopefuls. We'll confirm it as soon as it's leaked.

Moan factor: 4/10

Healthcare

★ Getting it out of our system ★

A nation of moaners has, of course, got a whole lot to say about health. Specifically healthcare and how we get it. And another H has to make a cameo here: hypochondria. We have plenty of real and imagined opportunities to put the system to the test.

Whether your ailment is real or not, you can add earache to the list when we get stuck into what's right or wrong with healthcare in this country. Very few countries have a solution for universal healthcare. But, here, we have a few techniques for upping the healthcare giving-out game.

* You are sicker than everyone else: It's not a cough, it's TB, and the doctor said you had the worst case she'd seen since she read about the Dublin tenements in history class.

* Eschew privacy at all costs: Tell everyone
  you're sick, how long you've been sick, how
  you got what you got and who you got it
  from. As ever, make sure to go on the radio
  and tell us all why your cold is the worst of all
  the colds ever, preferably before you consult a
  medical professional.

* Trolleys: You were on one, for a whole night,
  in a hospital corridor because they didn't have
  a bed for you? You must have gone private.

* Medical cards: You know the Golden Tickets
  in *Charlie and the Chocolate Factory*? That's what
  getting a medical card here is like. They seem to
  have even fewer these days than Willy Wonka
  sent out. Even if you're really ill, or a small child
  whose parents can't cope financially, you might
  as well eat some of Willie's chocolate. Then at
  least your tastebuds will feel better.

* Mental health: Nothing funny about this.
  So many Irish people suffer from some sort
  of mental health issue but stigma has kept
  us from giving out about it – even though it
  would have made us feel better and shown
  us we weren't alone. But Bressie off *The Voice*

raised awareness and now we're almost all on board and, as a bonus, we all think we can sing. This new openness is actually a bit worrying for the art of giving out: what if we all became so supportive that we all get happy and have to stop? Nah . . . Never happen. This is Ireland.

* Nurses: there will be the odd clichéd give-out about a nurse behaving badly in Copper Face Jacks with some guard some night, but mostly you wouldn't dare give out about them. (Note: pitch *Nurses Behaving Badly* to some lifestyle channel. It's obviously a fantasy show because nurses are great. Don't they deserve to let off some steam?) Wherever you go in the world, people talk at you for hours about how amazing Irish nurses are. How they work longer and harder than anyone else. How they are kind and make people feel special. Anyone who's ever had to deal with a vanishing consultant will know that it's the nurses on the ward who actually talk you through your diagnosis and are there for your and your family's care. So don't give out about our nurses. We just won't have it. What we can and should give out about? Their pay. It's insultingly rubbish.

'Oh, but the nurses love their work!' says Máiréad. 'They are *carers*. It's a vocation. They wouldn't choose to do anything else in life – this is what they were born to do.'

Feck right off, Máiréad. Let's take someone else's bonus and give it to them. Or make consultants earn theirs by wiping a few bottoms for themselves. They probably have a stash of wipes at the bottom of one of their many golfbags already.

Hey, consultants, wouldn't you feel so much better by the time you hit the eighteenth green if you'd *done* something?

Just a thought, Máiréad.

Moan factor: 10/10

Even though Scamall hates conventional medicine, she recently had to spend the night in A&E. She wrote to her local paper about it:

Dear Sir

As a regular contributor to this paper, you know I hate conventional medicine. I'm the kind of person who feels you should be able to heal yourself if society weren't poisoning us all and basically shooting at us with fluoride guns.

But society is poisoning us and so we have to pay The Man to see if he can make us better, when it's his fault we're sick in the first place.

I stick to a strict organic vegan diet, which is why I probably reacted so badly to the hotdog I had at the cinema the other night. (I normally wouldn't go to the cinema, but I couldn't miss the feature-length documentary about Ukrainian holistic collectives, Down at Heal, *and I'd urge everyone else not to either. It's four black-and-white hours that'll change your life.) Anyway, I would often forage when away from home, but I didn't want to miss a moment, so I ate what was available at the concession stand. I paid dearly for it – twice. First, it was nearly €7. Then it made me feel terrible. I got an agonising pain in my side so my friend Waft suggested I go to A&E. If the pain hadn't been so bad and the documentary nearly over, I'd have completely refused.*

And so I found myself in A&E with the great and the good and the bad of humanity. I'm the kind of person who thinks we're all equal but, honestly, the smell. And I don't shower that often, so I can put up with a lot.

There were queues and queues of people. I was down the list because my head wasn't pumping blood from falling down outside a nightclub (at least, that's where I assume all head injuries come from, I don't drink). So the staff couldn't see me. Waft had to go home after two hours so I was put on a trolley overnight. Then, they needed the trolley for someone who was 'dying' and the corridors were so full I was put in a flowerbed outside. Not a soft flowerbed, either: a shrubby one, practically a hedge. Now, I've campaigned for hedge preservation, but it's very hard to sleep in one when you're feeling off.

I wouldn't normally be the kind of person to complain, but I really felt terrible and nobody was free to help me. That's just not on.

As it turned out, it was just trapped wind. I won't tell you how I know but let's just say the wrens flew out of the hedge in the morning with some urgency.

But things could have been so much worse for me. And other people with worse injuries, of course.

I had to miss the end of a seminal film to not be treated by The Man. What the hell are we paying taxes for?

Love and light
Scamall de Spéir

Haterz Gonna Hate ... Ourselvez

★ Giving out about the givers-out ★

Soon we'll discuss how you're not supposed to give out about someone else's Irish Mother or Mammy (iMOM), although they themselves can. This is sort of similar, but with a bit of a patriotic twist.

If you're Irish and you give out about Ireland (which is practically our favourite thing) some old killjoys will swoop in and say it's 'self-loathing'. That pointing out our flaws, weaknesses or general tendencies amounts to paddywhackery, which, as we know, is *just the worst*. It's sort of like Ireland's Godwin's Law (where debate gets shut down by comparing aspects of the debate to Nazi Germany). No one wants to engage in paddywhackery when there aren't any tourists around to impress. The argument being that we're tacitly agreeing with an overseas cliché that Ireland isn't good enough.

Our view? These killjoys are missing the point. It's precisely *because we like ourselves* that we're able to take the piss. We do out of everyone else. Why not ourselves?

That said, phrases like 'self-loathing' appeal to our national sense of High Drama. In some ways, telling other people they're wrong not to be proud is a form of national pride. We get it.

But you can't be proud no matter what. It's just not logical. If your sister burns the house down, you can still love her, but it's okay to call the fire brigade. We've seen time and again that Ireland can't always be trusted with matches.

We all love Ireland, okay? It's just we know she could do so much better. We want her to know that, one day, she could have a boyfriend who treats her right. Tough love is something we do very well with here.

Besides, if you take away our giving out, what the heck are we left with?

Moan factor: 5/10

Tom, Seán, Máiréad, Scamall and (from his home studio) Ciarán take part in a televised Saint Patrick's Day forum (hosted by Jer, in a last-ditch attempt to get on telly) about what it means to be Irish today. Here are some highlights. It was a very long night. Most of it Máiréad:

Tom: 'Hello, Jer, nice to see you, and Happy St Pat's to ya! (Waves to camera, audience cheers.)
I think the Irish are brilliant, so we are. Still my favourite customers when they get into the cab and I don't mean anything by that. But you can have a laugh and a joke with them, y'know? And they always know where they're going. Ireland will be grand, so it will, so long as people have money for taxis and they keep going out. Isn't that right?' (Cheers.)
Scamall: 'Not everyone has money for taxis.'
Máiréad: 'It's nice to see fellows like Tom not ashamed of who they are or of being Irish and all

the rest of it. But I am, Jer. I'm ashamed. (Boos.) I'm sorry but I am. The country's changing too fast and it can't keep up with itself. We're losing sight of who we really are – God-fearing, decent people like I like.'

Scamall: 'Not everyone believes in God.'

Seán: 'All due respect to that first lady – Mary, was it? Máiréad. Máiréad, I'm sorry. All due respect to Máiréad, I'm a God-fearing man myself and I do like the way the country is going. Sure there's room for all of us. We have a great spirit about us, and I don't mind if someone finds that out through the God I believe in or by dancing around the fairy fort in my top field.' (Laughs.)

Scamall: 'Hear hear!'

Máiréad: 'Of course, and each to their own and all the rest of it, but without some form of structure, society falls apart. I mean, now that marriage is something that just anyone can do in this country, I don't know where to look. What will Ireland be in a few years? We don't know. We don't know. These changes may be quick, they may be slow, but soon we'll probably have communes and baby farms and that's just not the Ireland I recognise.' (Two people clap.)

Ciarán (via Skype): 'If I could just get in there, Jer. Thanks. Yeah, I mean, that lady doesn't realise it, but she's a McQuacker.'

Máiréad: 'A what? What's that now?'
Ciarán: 'You're a McQuacker. You wish we were all still living in caves, the way Bishop Whatsisname McQuaid wanted it.'

Scamall stands up and applauds. Her whole row looks even more uncomfortable than they already did.
Máiréad: (laughs) I do not indeed! I'm not like that at all. I've been known to watch soap operas and everything, even ones with some sex in them. You don't know me at all.'
Ciarán: 'OK, fine, whatevs. But, y'see, Ireland has moved on. You can either come with us, or be left behind. Bend or break, man. Bend or break.'

Scamall starts doing some chanting in Old Irish and plays the spoons on the studio steps.

Meanwhile Máiréad responds with a long, off-topic speech about how they do things in America (this only makes Scamall chant louder, to the dismay of the sound guys who are trying to mute her), and that time in Massachusetts where it all went horribly wrong. There's a long anecdote about her own sons and a skiing holiday and there may have been a recipe in there; no one's sure, they've all glazed over. Apart from Scamall's background chanting, no one interrupts Máiréad, for fear of being accused of silencing her. They know what she's like and they're over it. They just want it to end. Mere seconds before the credits roll, she finishes.

Máiréad: 'People need to be told what to do. It's worked for years. What it means to be Irish, to my mind, is basically to be a sheep. Aren't sheep well looked after? Fed, shorn, dipped occasionally? And brought back into the fold when they stray? But who's the shepherd now? Who's steering the ship? Who? (Theme music plays.) I will not be silen—'

Credits roll. Underneath, in the shadows, you can see Máiréad is still talking. Scamall seems to be in some kind of trance. But at least she's stopped playing the spoons.

Ratings for the show were the lowest on record for a Paddy's Day Special.

I is for . . .

iMOM

★ Updating Mammy ★

So we come to an Irish icon: the iMOM (Irish Mother or Mammy).

Máiréad is actually a pretty good example of an iMOM: capable, strong and a great multi-tasker – not to mention that she has the ability to drive you crazy half the time.

Along with fitting the traditional depiction of the Irish mother as the ultimate giver-out, selfless to the point of painful ('Don't mind me, I'll just sit here in the dark'), iMOMs are also modern women. That's why we've given them their snazzy new iMOM acronym.

iMOM might sound a bit like a robot, but sure aren't mammies programmed to do everything for us? (For their sons, anyway.)

iMOM:

* Is an expert at giving out. The wrath of an iMOM tops any other kind of wrath. (As Máiréád well knows, saying 'as a mother' in Ireland means you generally win.)

* Stores all your data (all of it, including bad memories and photos you'd rather had been destroyed).

* Reminds you of important dates (like the month's mind of that relative you never met).

* Is full of songs and stories. You'll never be bored with an iMOM around. She produces the food she knows you like, on plates exactly the right

temperature, like the computer in *Star Trek*.

＊ 'I'm grand' is her favourite phrase. We all
know what this means. They're not grand
at all. There is a draught. The tea isn't nice.
They're not having a lovely time and it's
the first thing they're going to tell all their
neighbours as soon as they get home – how
you dragged them up to Dublin and made
them have a horrible time doing stuff, but,
sure, they didn't say anything because
they love you. And you wondered why the
neighbours down home always gave you
an evil look as soon as you parked up your
conspicuous D-reg car? Now you know. You're
an awful child, which only serves to make
your iMOM all the more amazing.

＊ iMOMs have also mastered the unmasterable:
they manage to give out and not give out
about the same thing, at the same time. They
can communicate displeasure while seeming
to enjoy themselves. Even if they're not giving
out, something in their eyes will convey
constant disappointment, clearer than a 3-D
model of disappointment assembled in a
disappointment lab.

✳ But unlike her techno counterparts, the iMOM
   has a very long battery life and is completely
   waterproof. WE HEART iMOM.

From the way mammies have been depicted in the
past, you'd think we never give out about iMOMs. But
iMOMs are just so brilliant, reaching their standards is
impossible: you will never make a stew as great as hers,
or be as patient when it comes to people-managing on
some committee. iMOM will always do it better. That's a
lot of pressure. It's okay to give out about that pressure
because in it is implicit the wondrousness of iMOM.

   We learn everything we know from our iMOMs,
passive aggression being one of the very first lessons.
Just remember the cardinal iMOM rule, though: she's
allowed to moan about us; we're not allowed to moan
about her.* If we did, she has data we wouldn't want to
get out there.

   Where would we be without her?

   At a pinch – during an absolute *Jeremy Kyle*-style she-
ran-off-with-your-girlfriend highly unlikely pinch – you
are allowed to give out about your iMOM. BUT YOU
ARE THE ONLY ONE. If the iMOM in question is not
yours, here's the procedure:

---

* iMOM: who's allowed to give out.

* Outsiders have to keep their mouths shut at all times, bar when they're asked to try some of her cake. They must eat the cake, say it's nice and then shut their mouths again.

* Outside of cake niceness, outsiders must venture no further opinion on your iMOM, even to agree with something negative you've just said about her. NO. Even praise is out, because it shouldn't have to be said. Of course she's lovely. She's your iMOM. If YOU are criticising her (mildly, and only in a pinch), a friend can nod agreement, but must not stoke the fire or offer further reasons why she's awful. Even if she is being awful.

NB: The same applies to outsiders dissing extended family, your spouse, the pint in the local or Ireland.

Moan factor: 0/10

Tom the taxi driver sometimes recites some of his own poetry to his passengers:

'The twenty-first century's awful, isn't it? Place has gone to the dogs altogether, hasn't it? I have a poem about it. Would you like to hear it? Right, so.

1999 is in the rear-view mirror now
The price they sold the country off for, too
We all partied like 'twas then, but then 'twas over
And the clean-up took for ever, thanking you
The lady rode a tiger, then the tiger rode her back
And no one saw cos they were on their phone
I don't care about me brother, because I am all
right, Jack
So just leave me be, and leave me die alone.

'Ah, now, I never said it was uplifting! I'm just being honest. You have to tell it like it is, don't you? Where did you say you were going, again? The airport. Ah, sorry, love, I'm going the wrong way. I'll start the meter again.'

The Internet

★ The givers-out are out there ★

You might not get this impression from our donkey-filled postcards and insistence on banging on about the past, but we're fierce tech-savvy here. One of the only things you'll hear government spokespeople mentioning more than JOBS (see *JOBS*) is Wi-Fi (pronounced in exalted circles as 'Wiffy') and getting Wi-Fi to rural areas and making sure everyone has Wi-Fi because of JOBS.

Even before the twenty-first century really kicked in, we were one of the first countries to embrace the mobile phone ('we' meaning everyone, not just millionaires in soap operas). Tax incentives meant big tech companies came here and built tiny machines. Later, they shipped young people in brightly coloured sweaters with amazing eyewear and great laughs over here to great working conditions and – of course – the ubiquitous craic. Loads of them stayed and now young Irish people are also mad for tech and brilliant at it.

People under forty had computers at school and grew up not knowing there used not to be an internet. People over forty use it – like crazy, in fact – but still think it's some kind of witchcraft or voodoo. Ciarán has no time for them.

Ciarán – blogging as himself:

Technophobes (or 'olds') are nuts. As far as they're concerned, the internet is well dodge. Like they think it's spying on them and sending their awful flary photos around the world all by itself. Like anyone cares about their reflective thighs. They think the internet is trapping their grandkids somewhere called 'Skype': 'I thought they were in Australia. Waaah, the future, I'm scared!' Get a grip.

Worst of all, they don't like it bringing them into contact with people who don't agree with them, and the way communications are changing Ireland fast. It used to be a shitehole where nothing changed. From where I'm sitting, not being a shitehole is a good thing. Oh, and it's Wi-Fi. 'Wiffy' is how a shitehole smells.

So everyone chill, okay?

He's right about how it's changed Ireland. We were much easier to control before. No wonder the more traditional fear this warp-speed change. It came late but very quickly if you were in the middle of it. Control used to be easy: you'd just shushen people by taking away their earnings, or damning them for eternity and, sure enough, they'd all hunker down in their own parishes, miserable. Maybe there was some comfort in knowing where they stood. But then . . . but then . . .

Like some kind of big open window, the internet let us see that some of our more 'subversive' thoughts were maybe just 'thoughts'. That it was okay to question things. We began to speak our minds. We found like minds. Even better, we had access to all kinds of information – even the sexy kind – and realised there were other people out there *right now* who were being told to shush but wouldn't. It was great.

The internet helped facilitate Ireland's rollercoaster ride out of the Dark Ages to where we are today; maybe not the Bright Ages, but definitely brighter than before.

And now we can give out on a global scale, without even leaving our own homes. Result.

Moan factor: 3/10

Irregular Verbs

★ All grammar, no glamour: giving out about Gaeilge (Gaelic) ★

There are those who are fluent in our native (and, officially, first) language. Why wouldn't they be? It's beautiful. It's unique to us. It's impenetrable to almost anyone who hasn't heard it from birth: some of the ways you have to contort your vocal cords to get pronunciation just right require day-one training – like those tiny Eastern European gymnasts in the eighties.

But, largely due to the doom and gloom way it was taught to us – all reminiscences of old women and poems about TB – many of us just can't get our heads around it, much less our larynxes. Here are the fors and againsts our native tongue:

★

Giving Out Yards

TÁ	NÍL
✳ It's part of who we are.	✳ Or who we were.
✳ It means we can give out about people from other countries without them knowing what we're saying.	✳ We must admit, that's handy.
✳ It means we can give out about most people from our own country without them knowing what we're saying.	✳ Ditto.
✳ There's a ton of beautiful literature in Irish that just doesn't work in translation.	✳ But most of it is about death. Maybe if there were more dragons?
✳ The *Nuacht* (News in Irish) is on first, so Irish speakers are ahead of the topical curve.	✳ The News is bad in any language. We wish we didn't understand it at all, early or late.

Moan factor: Cúig/Deich

J is for ...

Judges

★ **Dealing with cute hoors and grand fellas altogether** ★

These are great fellas and women. They're very, very wise and well paid and some of them really do care about justice, which is great. As for patience, some of them should be given sainthoods for having to deal with cases such as the following:

* hedge claims

* bar managers who are too attractive for their customers to leave at closing time

* sons being bribed with iMOM-cooked meals to break restraining orders

* having to calmly repeat 'This isn't about surrogacy' approximately one million times during the Marriage Equality Referendum and to calmly explain how referenda worked when the outcome was challenged.

I mean, they probably got into judging to put bad guys away. It must get very tedious.

But this is Ireland and justice is a lot trickier – and plain cuter! – than elsewhere. But many judges are still part of the 'who you know' generation that had us fecked altogether. This means that if the defendant is known to them, it can have a bearing on the outcome of a case. Uh-oh! So cute!

As we know, Ireland's so tiny it's almost impossible to not know somebody. You've almost definitely snogged them in the Gaeltacht, snogged their cousin, or – if you're a judge – played golf with them on one of your many days off, exhausted from meting out justice, *then* snogged them. It's hard to be hard on someone if you've had a singsong with them. Understandable. Poor old judges. Such cute moral dilemmas.

In more than one recent rape trial, the sentences were suspended because the defendants had well-known local businesses or they were from overseas and we have to be nice to tourists, or something. We know, it does sound made up.

But let's look at the following possible-yet-fictitious scenario. Maybe the judge had to buy golf clubs from the defendant, and the golf clubs worked fine, so he believed the guy to be upstanding and decent and all. But whatever he believed, he knew him. He wouldn't want to shit on his own doorstep. Or golf bag. He'd probably be needing clubs again in future, after all.

And, sure, weren't the women involved absolutely fine now? It's not like they were sent to a Magdalene laundry or anything. They were free to come and go as they pleased, and if they didn't want to come across the defendant, all they had to do was avoid his shop/home country.

And if they were really uncomfortable in their homes, couldn't they move away? It's a free country. Especially if a judge knows you can recommend a great nine-iron.

By the way, we weren't privy to the judge's thought process, and the above is made up. However, this kind of sentencing – the 'He's a grand lad, really' method – happens more often than we'd like.

> Máiréad doesn't mind the 'he's a grand lad, really' method. She's always been a bit suspicious of women, to be honest. She called Jer:
>
> 'If a woman is the victim of a crime, it's usually best to assume that she is somehow to blame. I mean, how obvious were her breasts at the time? It's probably down to her own stupidity or the obviousness of her breasts. We deserve what we get! Life is full of suffering. It's why I always button my cardigan up to the top, Jer. (Laughs.) Then at least I know that whatever I did is not because I'm a stupid woman.'

If you're a woman and something is done to you, make sure you get a great defence lawyer for yourself. Everyone's a grand lad to someone. And grand lads have nothing to fear.

Moan factor: 9/10

Part 2 of the *Chronicle* story about Seán's hedge case. The verdict:

After lunch, Judge Michael Protestant passed sentence and not inconsiderable amounts of wind. Lawless, he said, had no business impersonating a sheep or any other kind of animal with the aim of gaining access to another man's hedge. However, he suspended Lawless' sentence due to it being 'a small world and life being too short'. He ordered him, quite crossly, never to do it again. Lawless nodded and all parties shook hands. Afterwards, all parties adjourned to the local, with sandwiches provided by Lawless' sandwich shop on Main Street.

When Is a Bridge Not a Bridge?

★ Green shoots! JOBS! Not really! ★

Q. When is a Bridge not a Bridge?
A. When it's a Job Bridge!

Oh, this is a fantastic idea, almost as good as the clamping. Whoever thought it up should get a prize because it's one of the only things holding this country together. That's right: JOBS.

Basically, it's a state-approved way to get yourself

some good old-fashioned child labour. Maybe not actual children, but no matter how they fancy it up, it still boils down to people being asked to work for nothing. Especially young people. Genius.

Now, you might say, 'Isn't that exploitative?', and the answer is, 'Yes.' Maybe, more accurately, 'It depends.' The employer gets an eager beaver who wants to prove themselves, who'll work harder for 'experience and training' than anyone ever did when these junior positions were paid ones. So they get to keep their business going and use the cash they've saved to go to restaurants and drive fancy cars and all those things that seem to make the government happy to point to them and say 'economic recovery', 'green shoots', 'turning the corner' and other meaningless phrases.

While their fingers are still out, the government then also gets to point to the live register and say JOBS. With the Job Bridgers technically 'employed', it looks great for all of us. Greenshootsrecoveryturningthecorner!

Moan factor: 3/10

Ciarán tweets:

Job Bridge? Knob bridge, more like. #amirite

Johnnies

★ Put a ring on it or tie a knot in it ★

No one really gives out about condoms any more, apart from late on a Saturday night when they won't come out of a vending machine quickly enough (although that beef is more with the dispenser than with the condom itself). But other than johnnies, you still can't really speak openly about contraceptives in Ireland without being seen to give out about them.

Condoms cause the least giving-out these days because (a) they're for guys, (b) AIDS and STIs are no craic and (c) back in the day, Gay Byrne once put one on a banana on *The Late Late Show* and they practically flew onto willies everywhere. If only you didn't basically have to be married or in the UK to get one at the time.

On ferries from Britain, while other tourists stuffed their cars with duty-free drink, young Irish men and women stuffed their pockets with condoms, sponges, caps – anything that would enable them to have responsible fun too.

Now, you can get the pill here – even the morning-after kind, much to Dev and ABJCMcQ's chagrin – and, for the most part, no one asks you for a marriage certificate or what you think you're doing with your life. You still risk the odd stern look, but it's worth it. It's for sex, after all. It's fun.

Now the giving out has moved from 'We won't have that sort of [widespread, wanton sex] here' to what's the best contraception for you or to what men would do if they had to take the pill. So, some of the heat has come off contraceptives, or shifted to areas like aborshhh . . . but they're still a talking point.

Traditional Irish contraception:

1. None, i.e. the best way: There are still those who'd prefer that we all got pregnant every time, like we're supposed to.

2. Restraint: This is the second best way.

3. Something involving calendars and thermometers: There's so much faffing that you'll be way too tired to be horny.

4. A sexy pep talk from a person of the cloth: You'll probably never have sex again.

5. Have kids: There's no better ardour cooler than the prospect of eighteen years of making school lunches and going to under-16 GAA matches in the rain. But, then, some people like rain. They just seem to want everyone else to get wet, too.

Moan factor: 2/U16

Máiréad wrote to her local pharmacist about contraception:

Dear McMahon's Pharmacy

First, let me welcome you to the area. It was a shame when Murphy's closed down but I'm glad to see you've not only refitted the shop, but kept it as a chemist's, which is great for the town. A cough can easily develop into pneumonia unless you're wearing a vest. Supermarket cough syrup isn't as effective. You'd need the chemisty stuff. I'll be in to you for some soon, no doubt, despite my daily vest-wearing habit.

However, I would like to make you aware of how Murphy's used to do things, which kept us all cough-free and happy for over forty years. Each to their own and all the rest of it, but there's no point changing things now.

I was in your shop the other day and I was in shock following the following incident.

I overheard a young woman asking for emergency contraception. Emergency? She had had plenty of time to think about what she was about to get up to the night before, so to call it 'emergency' makes a mockery of the English language.

Now, I was expecting that she would be chastised

and sent packing, as normal, or given the standard leaflet showing the most compassionate ferry times to England. Instead, your employee treated her with kindness! I could hardly believe my eyes. She took her aside into a room where I trusted she was telling her (a) to get married (there was no ring on her left hand), (b) to cop on to herself or (c) to abstain, like I do. You can't get pregnant from doing nothing. It works.

Imagine my disgust when they emerged from the private room (from which I could hear nothing, by the way: Murphy's curtain arrangement was much better) and when they did, they were smiling. Smiling! The customer got her prescription filled and off with her into her day as if I'm not allowed to have a say in it at all.

Mr Murphy – God rest him – would have had the decency to shame the girl in front of the whole shop so she and everyone else would realise she was wasting her life and it'd put any prospective suitors off. That would have taught her.

I like the new front you've put on the shop. Let that be the end of the modernising you do.

Yours,

Máiréad

★

K is for . . .

Kids

★ Children, the gloves are off ★

We love kids. We do! Even more than we love babies, who are similar to kids only smaller and easier to store, and as they don't need shoes yet, they work out less expensive. Let's have a look at what life in Ireland is like for these little guys in the years between birth and Job Bridge or Emigr8ion.

Basically, outside their immediate family, by kid-stage most people will have lost interest. No longer babies, they're slightly less cute and harder to store. Even the state and 'pro-family' people don't seem concerned by this stage. The families of these kids are expected *not* to ask for *anything* now: e.g. childcare that isn't a luxury item, a choice in religious or secular education, somewhere other than a car to sleep, shoes, better storage – you name it. The truth is we don't really seem to want to know.

All the more hypocritical given that if you don't have kids in Ireland – especially if you're a woman – you're subject to some pretty gruelling talkings-about. They'd prefer to burn you at the stake, but they'll settle for the talkings-about-behind-your-back, which can burn almost as badly.

If you don't like being pitied or the subject of scathing looks, it's probably easier to just go ahead and have the kids. As many as you can manage. More than you can manage, preferably. Then you'll fit right in.

Possibly the worst thing about being a kid in Ireland is that you have to audition for *The Late Late Toy Show*.* It's compulsory. Even if you don't make it through to the actual show, your try-out will be shown to the nation during the 'dregs' segment, with your version of 'Jingle Bells' dubbed over by that of a more talented child.

Yeah, being a kid in Ireland isn't great. Just remember: you're never too young to apply for your own passport.

Moan factor: 1 (seen)/ 10 (but not heard)

Kin-sternation

★ We are not all extras in your episode of *Who Do You Think You Are?* ★

We'll look at Ireland-based family in *Theory of Relativity*. But in *Kin-sternation*, we give out about the Irish abroad who come here looking for their roots.

What with all the hot emigration and diaspora action, no matter where you were born on the planet, there is someone in Ireland related to you and waiting with bated breath for your triumphant return to tell them

---

* See *The Late Late Show*.

how great you're getting on overseas. Good for you. We're delighted.

Gag.

You'll have realised by now that, of course, we're giving out about you. We know you're excited to hear the family history, but let us save you some time.

An Irish family tree stretches back from the present more or less like this:

Farmer
↓
Farmer
↓
Teacher
↓
Farmer
↓
Farmer
↓
Farmer
↓
Secret Priest
↓
Farmer
↓
Farmer
↓
Farmer
↓
Farmer
↓
Farmer
↓
Chieftain (no one is really descended from a chieftain, but we've all made up at least one.)

Because families have traditionally been so big (see *Theory of Relativity*) it's only possible to remember seven key family-member names at any one time, after which pointing, nodding and mumbles come into play. It's too much to expect one human to be able to remember how thousands of people – many of them dead – are supposed to interrelate. Some of the older rellies can do it because all they have to keep in their heads are those names and a few memories of a simpler time, like not having to lock their bikes.

Outside these elders, the American Kin are your best bet. We're constantly amazed at what they know about family history. Or that they care. They get off the plane at Shannon and dash straight to the coat-of-arms place, not even stopping for the mandatory medieval banquet on the way (they'll catch it on the way back). They know more about heraldry than the guy in the place. True, they may add to your burden of 'Oh, Christ, more cousins' but if you're wise, you won't shut them out, even if this means showing them around graveyards and heraldry places and pubs full of carts: they care about this malarkey and have learned off *all* the names. They are invaluable. Keep them close.

Don't judge us, Overseas Kin! Living here surrounded by the past all the time gets a little in your face; we have to tune out sometimes. It's not that we're not interested in being related to you: you might turn out to be very wealthy, after all. But we will never jump up and down in graveyards with the same fervour as you do.

Moan factor: 3/10

Kit Off

★ Naked un-ambition ★

As observed earlier, we don't see a lot of bare flesh here because of flare issues and bushels of shame. For a long time, we all had to pretend we were born with clothes on us. And so, unless you're a retired judge, jumping balls-out into the Forty Foot, nakedness causes a lot of giving out there. For example:

1. 'She was prancing around the changing room, boobs to the wind. Hussy.'

2. 'All the women are wearing summer dresses around town. It's a distraction to drivers and very unsafe.'

3. 'They'd a sauna. In their house, like. Disgusting.'

4. 'There was a programme on there where an Irish woman took her top off. She wasn't even in need of resuscitation, so this was very far-fetched.'

5. 'I know she was breastfeeding, I know, Jer. But I was having my lunch.'

It's a shame, because our pagan ancestors loved a bit of naked celebration. And it really cut down on your getting-ready time for an event.

Moan factor: 0/ 10 (It never happens)

$\mathcal{L}$ is for . . .

Literature

★ Every day we (don't) write the book ★

Everyone in Ireland has written, or is writing, a novel. You can take this as read. Not the novel, of course, because this hasn't been written yet and never will be. This makes us very defensive. You have a great story in you but you don't have the time/an atmospheric writing attic/a working pen. Or you *do* have a day job/a family/inertia/a bottomless well of excuses.

Be sure to be really bitter and give out about all the things getting in the way of your writing your book. Give out yards about it all the time and sneer at other writers who are getting the words down on paper and out into the world.

As far as we're concerned, having our piece of this country's rich literary history is our birthright. As such, we have a list of literary demands. Because we are genii, we expect this won't be a problem.

* We should be given publishing deals at sixteen, the way Americans are given cars. (Yeah, we watch MTV).

* Corners of pubs should be cleared for us on our arrival.

* A reverent hush should descend as we enter with our ink pot and quill.

* Pints of whiskey should be served by grateful bartenders and paid for by loving admirers.

* The Wi-Fi should *always* be free – a man with an aerial should follow us around to make sure; we don't know how Wi-Fi works – we're so delightfully scatty.

* We should automatically be invited on *The Late Late Show* to promote our latest blog post.

* We should be carried shoulder height down Grafton Street when we get too tired to walk; the finger-and-eye-strain is a killer.

* We should be invited to all the awards and win most of them.

* We should get fellowships at the world's universities and, as we guest-lecture at the Sorbonne, people should whisper, 'Not just

a writer . . . an *Irish* writer!' excitedly to each other, in French.

So when we inevitably don't get the acclaim *that is our birthright* for our every written word (or every word we really, really intend to write), of course we give out about it.

If only we did that giving out on paper. Maybe then the Nobel panel would take note.

Moan factor: Joyce/Behan

Scamall blogs on procrastination:

I have been writing my novel Underground Coven *for about three years now. I'm hoping to get it finished soon, but it's based on my local coven, so very true to life, and life takes as long as it takes. I've really had to immerse myself and get down with my inner witch. A bit of nudity, a lot of herb-gathering. That's no problem for me. I'm the kind of person who lives in the moment so immersing is kind of my thing.*

People think that – because I don't work, as they see it – I have a lot of time on my hands but I don't really. I need a lot of sleep because I burn off a lot of mental energy meditating and interacting with other people's creative auras. You can't get down with all that unless you live it. And writing can be heavy: you have to give it its organic space. You have to make choices and decisions, and a character's life could depend on it. Their life, man. So you have to put the downtime in.

I write every day, so that mind-muscle is constantly flexed. I write blogs (like this one) and tweets and mulch-letters. So, really, I'm just waiting for my book's world to reveal itself – maybe in a dream. Then I'll just be setting down what's already written in my head. Underground Coven is going to be awesome. I'm going to write a chapter today. Definitely. Right after I forage up lunch.

Comments have been disabled.

Love

★ All will not be revealed ★

It's no secret that we Irish like to keep things close to our chests, although you'd never know it from how much we give out in public. We're happy to gossip and give out about neighbours and in-laws or pontificate about how Dennis down the road should live his life. ('He always had that bowel problem. It's what has him the way he is.')

No detail of someone else's life is too intimate. But when it comes to revealing something about our own emotional lives, we get very uncomfortable. *Veeery* uncomfortable altogether.

And so those three little words are extremely hard for us to say. One of the most popular ways to say 'my love' in Irish is 'a *rún*' – 'secret'. Even if the relationship isn't clandestine in any way. It's just that love isn't really something you'd be bragging about; it's something you keep to yourself. Even from the object of your affections. They're the last person you should be letting on to.

Here, we express love by hanging around the person a lot and hoping they notice. This starts behind the bike shed at school and continues until a few years into a marriage.

Saying 'I love you', aloud, is another of those things seen as a bit 'American'. Deep down inside, we love hearing it. It touches us; we have to turn to wipe away the tears. But outwardly we have to pretend that the sayer of the words is a bit of an eejit and definitely 'soft' or 'daft'. Such a person will probably expect an awful lot from you in return, like you voicing your feelings aloud as well.

Divorce is only a couple of decades old here so many still have the real expectation that marriage will definitely be for life – long past the romance stage. That means declarations of love are seen as sappy, un-businesslike and maybe even a small bit false. 'Get out of that!' you'll say, thumping your spouse on the arm to reinforce the fact that you once had a physical connection. 'You big eejit.'

In fact, 'you big eejit' could almost be said to be our three little words.

Moan factor: 1/10 (Any more would be giving it away)

The Late Late Show

★ To whom it concerns, it's still on ★

In other countries, TV shows generate water-cooler moments. Something you wish you hadn't missed or were delighted you didn't miss and you can't wait to talk to someone else about. Here, of course, we're after the opposite. What we want are giving-out opportunities.

So how lucky are we that our national TV station's flagship show is essentially a museum piece from the fifties, running pretty much unchanged every weekend since then?

To much loud giving-out, it switched from Saturday to Friday, and there have been different presenters and wildly varying topics. Otherwise, nothing's changed. Some even suspect that the same audience has lived in the studio since the start, bedding down under the seats along with next week's spot prizes. Oh, the things they've seen. Condoms being put on bananas. Bono being put on a bike. Audience prizes from cars to knitting patterns. Literally all of human (and sometimes animal) life is there.

Remember when you were a kid and you went to a museum but you didn't really want to go? But when you actually got there you realised that, while a lot of it was dusty, and should never have been brought out of the store-room, some of it was shiny and cool? Some of it was enjoyable scary, with big, snarly, exposed teeth. And some of it reached national-treasure status. Well, the *Late Late* is exactly like that: you have a certain degree of duty to visit but once you're in, if you hang on, there just might be something of interest to you.

No two people will ever agree on a particular episode: one person's 'This is really relevant, more of this!' is another's 'Why is that fella on again? This show is a relic!' They're both right.

One of the only things every single Irish person on the planet agrees on – in general, not just about telly – is that you all have to watch *The Late Late Toy Show* every Christmas. But aside from that one magical evening of grown-ups playing on too-small bikes and children singing inappropriately grown-up songs, the *Late Late* continues to confound us. And remember, kids, keep practising. You DO NOT want to end up on the 'dregs' reel.

REAL FACT

The Late Late Show is over at eleven. We can't even agree on what 'late' is.

Moan factor: 1950/10

The Local

★ Where everybody knows your name . . . and what you give out about ★

We don't give out about our local: that's tantamount to sacrilege. Rather, it's a cathedral of giving out. And we are all the archbishop of it.

As we know, Irish people love a religious experience. Somewhere we can congregate and commune, and indulge in rituals in a sacred place. When that ritual is giving out, the local is the perfect spot.

Your 'local' is 'your' pub. You may not be lucky enough to own one, and it may not be the one geographically closest to your home, but if the bartenders know you and you get a right old slagging when you walk in, it's definitely your local. It's where everybody knows your name . . . and practically everything else about you. Especially the things you love to give out about.

In smaller towns and villages, finding a local can be tricky. These are jealously guarded spaces. Someone who's taken a set against you might feel it's more their local than yours. Tough where there's only one pub – but there are absolutely no towns or villages with only one pub so you're safe there. Even if there are only two houses, there'll be more than one pub.

If somebody feels you're a bit of a blow-in, they'll give out about you and how this can never be your local because you're 'not from around here'. You might have been frequenting this same pub for forty years, but if they've been going there for forty-one, they'll feel justified. The local doesn't have to be fancy: it might be the kind of place where a sigh comes out of the tap before the stout does. It just has to be somewhere with a stool for you to feel comfortable venting on. Your giving-out home-from-home.

Your local will be the place you'll do most of your one-on-one, face-to-face giving out (and be given out about too, don't you worry). Locals are like a 3-D internet, comments flying right and left. Or mass, but a mass where you all get a go at being the priest, pontificating and sermonising to a rapt congregation.

Before Bressie made talking about mental health cool, your local was your therapy, too. Better even than confession. You could bare your soul, not get any penance and then get chips on the way home. And if you felt in any way uncomfortable afterwards about having overshared, everyone would pretend you hadn't said it at all, or pat you on the back and say, 'Ah, you were drunk!' as if that shifted time and made the thing unhappen. Lovely.

Moan factor: 0/10 (1/10 only if a tourist manages to nab your favourite seat)

ℳ is for . . .

Mortgage
★ Or Lessage ★

As part of the whole finance-and-property-ladder debacle (see *Finances* and *Rung Up*), these were the must-have accessory of 2004 (mortgages and €400 shoes, which young people came to believe was just the price of shoes). Some mortgages were big, some were small – wait, who are we kidding? They were *all* enormous.

Obviously that had (and continues to have) a horrible knock-on effect on rent, as landlords struggle to pay for their house-shaped clutch handbags. It's really lucky so many people enjoy the outdoors (see *Camping in the Streets*).

But you really stuck out back then if you didn't have a mortgage. You'd do whatever you had to to get one, but the truth was, you didn't have to do anything. The banks were hauling people in like the Child Catcher from *Chitty*

Chitty Bang Bang, handing out 100 per cent mortgages instead of lollipops. We wouldn't have fallen for lollipops. We're not that stupid. Although that's debatable, because lollipops are delicious.

Talk about buyer's remorse! In 2008 everything went to hell and we all got kicked in the eye and realised all we were left with were massive piles of bricks, massive piles of no-savings and massive piles of no-future. Plenty to give out about there: massive piles of it. Mind you, we'll never get into a horse-drawn wagon with a strange bank man again, we swear.

Not that he'll have a horse-drawn wagon. He'll have a shiny new car. And a big €400 boot - all the better to kick us in the eye.

Moan factor: 10/10

Ciarán blogging as **Slyfox99**:

HOPE ALL FASCISTS ARE HAPPY W/ THERE MORTGAGES!!! U RUINED THE COUNTRY SAME AS IF U DROPPED US OFF A CLIFF. U R COLLUDIN IN A CAPITALIST FANTASY N I HOPE THE PAINT PEELS OFF UR 08 BEEMER ASAP. DAT'S ALL U CARE ABOUT. IF I RULED THIS COUNTRY, I WUD OPEN D DOORS TO D VAULTS N LET EVERYONE HELP THEMSELVES. EVERYTHING WUD BE FREE N THERE WUD BE NO MORE TAXES. IF PEOPLE

DIDN'T LIKE IT I WUD MARCH THEM OFF A CLIFF. FASCISTS.

Moving Statues

★ Holy shows ★

We can't really explain why, like holy golf courses, we've had so many apparitions and moving holy statues per head of the population. Some people truly believe they're heavenly messages. Some give out that they're cynical, pilgrim-enticing exercises, contrived to get money out of the faithful somehow.

Huge in the eighties, 2015 saw the thirtieth anniversary of the Our Lady who kicked it all off: the moving statue of Ballinspittle.

Apparitions still occur occasionally, up and down the country, mostly in the form of a moving Mary or . . . Well, actually, it's almost always her. She seems to have adapted a use-it-or-lose-it policy when it comes to mobility. No wonder she looks so good in all the religious art.

It's definitely an Irish thing: in other formerly staunchly Catholic countries, they're nowhere near as popular. The market overseas seems a lot more niche. The other aspect of this that sets us apart is that apparitions and messages get prime, unchallenged state-broadcaster coverage. If you hear a serious radio programme detailing the latest arrival of Holy Mary in a wardrobe, it's probably not a spoof. No, no. What's going into your ears there is real reportage.

Ireland is renowned for its tourism, so I suppose we shouldn't really be surprised that Mary and Jesus and the lads want to come here for a visit, too. Or that people who want tourists to come might want to encourage that idea. With their flowing robes and beards the holy gang would have fitted right in with the other tourists here in the seventies, then again in the late nineties when the seventies were back in, and at every festival since.

In their heyday, the apparitions were everywhere – almost like a more saintly version of the showbands that toured the country in vans, leaving no village hall without a hop. They've appeared on hillsides, on the sides of churches, at the site of a soon-to-be airport as well as in gardens and in people's minds. They leave detailed and complex messages, like 'Lo, build ye an airport here. Yes, in the middle of nowhere. Do not question I, who am currently appearing on the gable end of a house.'

When local holy statues started moving in the eighties, suddenly everyone could be a visionary. You didn't even need the mess or fuss of stigmata or miracles, the crowds would still come Once the Ballinspittle statue set the shaky trend, it brought pilgrims and news crews from around the world. Experiments were done to see if the perceived movement was down to natural gas, or an electrical fault in the halo lights, which seemed to strobe if you looked at them for ages.

Seán was at Ballinspittle in 1980. He talks to Jer:

'I'd a lovely experience there. I thought maybe I might meet some nice girls. Well, there were loads, but they'd no interest. They were all looking up at the hill. It was like a Michael Jackson concert. There she was, herself, the BVM, moving away. Well, not doing the Moon Walk or anything. But the lights on her halo were strobing away, as if she was nodding her head. I never saw anything like it.

'Like any big gig there was a lot of fainting so the local GPs parked up on site. I was kicking myself I wasn't cute enough to park up myself and sell cups of tea for the shock. Someone said there were ten thousand people there every night. Imagine selling ten thousand cups of tea! I'd have made a fortune! Sure I could have got rid of the cattle then, only I love what I do. And I did think to myself that even Jesus would have had a hard time making fish sandwiches stretch to that number.

'Anyway, you could hear the hymns and rosaries all the way up in Cork.

'There was a new phone box there so you could call home if you had an experience. I rang Mammy and told her it was probably worth making the trip. On the way home, I stopped into the paper shop and bought her *Ballinspittle at Night*, a tape of the people on the hill praying and singing 'The Bells of the Angelus'. Well, she only loved it. But I did think to myself that that, now, was probably an even better money spinner than the tea.'

Unfortunately, as far as we know, *Ballinspittle at Night* is no longer available. It's a real thing, though. A new version has been touted, but the equipment would have to be very sensitive in order to pick up just two devout people praying at the foot of a slope.

Moan factor: 7/10

Mammy (See iMOM)

But seeing as we're here . . .

You're Not the Mam of Me: A Special Note on the iMOM-In-Law

★ I fought the in-laws and . . . well, you know the rest ★

An iMOM is nothing compared to an iMOM-in-law:

that's iMOM squared, right there. That's a heck of a lot of judgement. No matter what happens, it's the in-laws' fault (i.e. yours), coming in here with their strange new ideas.

The relationship between iMOMs and their sons is a thing to behold. Do not get in the way of that relationship. iMOMs are the high priestesses of giving out, and their sons can do no wrong. (Irish daughters just don't get the same adulation, so if your partner's a woman, congratulations. No one will care.)

From the moment you give her son the glad eye in a shop, or somewhere, iMOM-in-law will detect you as a kind of wall being installed between her and her beloved baby boy. You are coming for him, changing him. Here are just some of her fears:

* You will make him have sex for the very first time (*he's thirty-five*).

* This will make him want to leave home (*he hasn't lived there for years*) to have more of it with you, louder.

* He'll become one of those vegetarians, wanting nut roasts or whatever they eat for the Sunday dinner and nobody knows what goes in them, so she'll have to take a cookery course now so that her nut roast can be the best nut roast.

* You will make him move up to Dublin (*he's lived there since the late nineties*).

* You will make him drive too fast, with all that sex-tosterone going to his head.

* You will make him a parent (*as is your duty*), making her a grandiMOM before she's even ready, and she'll have to work out even harder at Pilates so that people will say they can't believe it. Basically, you make her very, very nervous.

There is only way to deal with this: presents. Always, always bring presents and never stop. These will still be given-out about when you leave, but at least your husband's father can interrupt a particularly suspicious rant with 'Now, love, she/he did bring that lovely lamp . . .' It will be enough to silence her for about three and a half minutes. Take it.

Moan factor: High drama/10

Máiréad on her new daughter-in-law:

'It was almost a lovely wedding, Jer. Almost. If she'd only listened – sure I was only trying to help! First, they wanted to have it outside. The ceremony. Outside. That's just crackers. Sure, you're too far from an altar for any blessing to even stick. Next, they said that they didn't even want a blessing! They wanted one of those celebranty people, under a tree. I mean, what are we – pagans? Well, at that stage, I put my foot down, Jer. Each to their own and all the rest of it but no son of mine was getting married unless it was in a church. I reminded them gently that they'd only be married in the eyes of the law, and what good is that to me the next time I see Fr Brennan? What would I say? That we thought his blessing was inferior to that of some leaf-waving charlatan? Honestly, love makes people eejits. Marriage isn't for eejits, Jer, or I'd never have done it.

'I told them to cop on to themselves and have it in the church or I'd go for one of my very long walks. They all know what that means (laughs): 'Unleash the dogs of war!' Not that Fluffy could ever be mistaken for a war dog, but I don't get rid of aggression on my walks you see, Jer: I sort of build it up. Then I can really let rip when I get home.

'Anyway, my son comes to me and says they'll get married in a church. Herself was off in the bedroom crying, but that's no harm because life is full of suffering and you may as well use your wedding as a trial run. In the end, Fr Brennan did a lovely mass. Oh, it was beautiful. I was delighted. I didn't even mind that I wasn't sat at the top table.'

Man's Best Friend's Worst Bits

★ The scoop on dog poop ★

There are two kinds of Irish dog-owner: those who pick up after their dogs and those who don't. They each have various reasons to give out.

Those who do pick up say	Those who don't say
✳ If dogs had opposable thumbs, they'd do it themselves.	✳ I don't know where you buy the little bags.
✳ Never let it be said that I contributed to the ruining of someone else's shoes or day.	✳ Damned if I'm walking around with one of those scoop yokes. Sure, everyone would think I thought I was some kind of fancy American.

★

* Maybe if more of us picked up, they'd take down those weird posters of the child with the big red circles in their eyes. I had nightmares last time I saw it.

* It's natural. If God had intended us to pick up, He'd have put some kind of collection system under the dog's arse.

* I don't want an on-the-spot fine. It's not fair on Spot.

* Nobody picks up my shite, why should I do it for a dog?

And then there are those who say that such controversy between dog-owners wouldn't occur if dogs weren't allowed anywhere in the first place. They just give out about dogs in general.

1. They're dangerous.

2. If they're too cute, they take the focus away from humans.

3. Bad ones kill sheep, which makes them almost as terrifying as gulls.

4. We're all allergic to them really.

5. They're child substitutes and more people would be pregnant only for them.

6. They bring mud in.

7. They prevent burglaries, taking business away from ordinary decent criminals and forcing them into other criminal areas, like drugs. It's all dogs' fault.

And there you thought they were just fluffy companions. In truth, by giving us so much to give out about, dogs really are man's best friend.

Moan factor: K9/10

N is for . . .

Neighbours

★ **Does everybody really need them?** ★

MADE-UP SAYING

If absence makes the heart grow fonder, nearness makes you cray-cray.

That saying may be made up, but in the case of the people we see every day, it fits. You'd have to be a little mean about certain neighbours to keep you sane enough to endure the proximity.

MADE-UP FACT

Long ago, very very few unrelated Irish people lived near each other.

A household (Irish: *teaghlach*) itself was big: you married into a *teaghlach*, had children under that roof, stayed on to look after the old folks and so it continued. But in rural areas (which almost all areas were in olden times) you mightn't see anyone else outside that household for months at a time.

If we're honest, despite loving the craic, Irish people can be pretty solitary creatures. When that craic was squished out of us, we grew more suited to living halfway up a mountain or in the middle of a bog and only surfacing for Christmas mass, the local or, when necessary, to sell a cow. (We've all read *Peig*.) The Shushening made us a little awkward around other people, which is possibly why many of us need to be drunk to start speaking to others, let alone start touching or embarking on relationships.

Long ago, neighbours used to drop in and you'd all have the times together: telling ghost stories (which we invented), singing badly and drinking tea fair wiled away the pre-*The Voice* evenings. But was it all really that cosy? Oh, you'd pretend you were happy the neighbours had dropped in unexpectedly, but really you'd be miffed you hadn't time to tidy the gaff, or hide stuff. You'd really want them gone ASAP.

MADE-UP FACT

The reason for the invention of ghost stories was to frighten them off in the hope that they'd have such bad nightmares when they got home that they'd never come back. Likewise, like an early *The Voice*, the singing would be terrible, outstay its welcome, and everyone would have to listen with their backs turned to spare the awful singer embarrassment. Anything to make sure that these casual dropper-inners didn't drop in casually again. Although they inevitably did. All the time. Telly couldn't come quickly enough.

Now many of us live in non-bog situations and have awkwardly had to accept the presence of neighbours. Ones we can't just sing away, because they live in the apartment next to us. We are improving, though, now The Shushening is finally beginning to recede in the rear-view.

Giving Out Yards

Sometimes we almost forget our awkwardness. But at others, while we smile and nod and hug, we may secretly be thinking up ghost stories.

Those who do pick up say	Those who don't say
* They're there when you need a cup of sugar.	* Really? When was the last time anyone outside a US sitcom did this?
* They're there when you need a cup of anything, really.	* And still there when you want to keep the news about what you've run out of to yourself.
* They water your plants when you go away.	* And probably try on your Y-fronts. And laugh.
* It's nice to chat over the hedge.	* So long as the hedge isn't the subject of a boundary dispute.

* They were very nice about that party you had.

* Yeah, because you had to give in and invite them, just in case.

* If someone were to break in, they could hear your cries for help.

* They can hear your every whisper. To be honest, you'd have more privacy if someone did break in.

* They know everything about you: you don't have to explain.

* They know everything about you: you don't have to explain.

Moan factor: 3/10

Nuns

★ A hard habit to break ★

You hear a lot about priests, so we're going to have a look at what the sisters were doing for themselves.

With the grip of The Shushening loosening on Ireland, this may seem like a retro topic. But we couldn't leave 'the penguins' out. They used to be really terrifying. Especially the teaching ones. And the orphanage ones. And the ones who mistook septic tanks for meadows.

Many of them were great, but there's no point messing about: for a lot of them, the power went straight through the veils and into their heads. Some of them made Nurse Ratched look like Glinda the Good Witch of the South. It's time to give out a bit about them.

Nuns used to rule the roost, like terrifying giant black and white penguiny chickens. They were the only penguiny hens in town for education and salvation if you were a sinner, which of course – according to them – everyone was. It was hard to know how not to be a sinner bar becoming a nun yourself. They themselves did stuff you were fairly sure were sins but they were nuns, so you were wrong: everything they did was holy. Or so they told us. It was all very confusing.

You couldn't leave a baby with a sinner (or, as the Church called sinners, 'women') so the nuns took the babies away. But let's skim over all that, because it's just too depressing and hard to digest. Ireland has indigestion. No wonder we give out.

But perhaps the cruellest thing the nuns ever did was to let kids have school discos. WHY? All it achieved was high blood pressure for themselves and confirmation to the kids of what sinners they were. There ain't no boner-killer like an eighty-year-old nun hurling herself between two over-sexed teens shuffling to 'Careless Whisper'. Many haven't touched another person since. Probably never will.

The Eighties: The Last Gasp

The eighties also saw a fairly heavy recruitment drive. Even by then, the pep talks were too late: young girls had already seen *Working Girl*. We knew we could maybe one day get jobs in high-powered offices and bump into Harrison Ford in the lift. We liked Day-glo colours: we didn't fancy spending the rest of our lives in black. And the abuse stories were just starting to come out; that wasn't great. People legged it out of mass in droves – even when the priests tried to jazz up the services by doing sermons about *Dallas* – so you'd have been hard pressed to drag them into a convent.

Most of us know we aren't sinners now. And we're cross about all that time we were told we were.

Inside many people raised in Holy Catholic Ireland there rages an *Incredible Hulk*. Each new post-Shushening revelation means our Hulk vein throbs, our fists clench, and we can only hope our trousers don't split. They made us angry. Now they don't like us when we're angry.

Moan factor: 8/10

> Máiréad rings Jer in a tizzy, after the bodies of 800 babies are found in a convent septic tank. (WE KNOW: NOT FUNNY AT ALL.)

'The thing is, Jer, people are very quick to judge. There's probably a perfectly reasonable explanation. Those babies could have all gone for a walk and got lost down the sewer. Or it might be some kind of underground baby colony. Or prehistoric alien eggs. Why do people hate religion so much that they assume they come from the adjacent convent? There was an orphanage there, sure, but in all the photos of the time the babies are alive. So where's the proof?

Eight hundred is a very big number, so I'm certain it was made up. Besides, there were only six hundred children in Ireland in total,* so this figure is impossible. Each to their own and all the rest of it, but this is anti-Catholic, Jer, and going to these

---

* Máiréad has done a made-up fact here herself and not flagged its makey-uppiness.

ridiculous lengths to make the Church look bad is
not funny.'

Nope. Not funny at all.

The News

★ Very serious altogether. If you've heard of us ★

Good evening, here is the News. It's at nine, unless it's at
six, in which case it's at 6.01 due to the perpetual bonging
of the Angelus. (See *The Bongs, The Bongs.*)

The News in Ireland is always bad. And if it isn't, don't
worry, we'll still find a way to give out about it. Even if
they do one of those funny 'kitten in a tree' items at the
end, it'll be followed by a terrible weather report to bring
you right back down to earth with a bump.

No harm, really, because with austerity (don't say it),
water-charge shenanigans, child poverty, repossessions,
cuts, football corrup-urrgh – we can't even finish – the
News would have you climbing up the tree after the
kitten, just to get away from it all.

Serious, serious issues come out of our papers, TVs,
radios and neighbours' mouths all day long. Ireland
has loads of news! Loads of reasons to give out! It's all
very serious! But then you go abroad and realise no one
reports on us, ever, unless we make a really big mess of

things or do something utterly history-makingly brilliant. If we didn't traditionally mess up quite a bit or win the Eurovision sometimes, no one would have heard of us. Overseas, we're not even as notable as local kittens. And when you're trumped by a small American cat – even when there's been an earthquake in Wexford, AN EARTHQUAKE – you realise you're not that globally significant.

There have been some complaints lately that the News focuses on what the News wants to focus on, and not what's actually happening out there on the streets. As at least one of us has usually been passing when the thing was happening, we get very annoyed if it's left out. Do you remember when your birthday didn't scroll across the screen on Saturday-morning shows when you were little? Like that, only more serious. You can't get away with not reporting stuff here because we all know about it anyway. We all live nearby.

We *are* the News: cuts, hospital trolleys, history-making referenda – we're living it and filming it on smartphones. There's no point trying to leave it out. You only look like eejits if you do.

And now the weather. (Actually, it's a bit later, under W.)

Moan factor: 6.01/10

★

O is for . . .
Outrage

★ Why give out about a molehill if we can make a mountain of it? ★

Our love of giving out means we have plenty of it, and caller-driven shows will never, ever be stuck for material. Someone somewhere in Ireland right now is outraged and wants to talk about it. They might be sitting next to you on the bus. They might be you. Don't make you angry: you wouldn't like you when you're angry. As you know.

Truth be told, we love it when someone else is angry. It's fantastic entertainment. We all accept that soon it will be our turn to blow our top and give someone else a great show. Like national service, everyone has to do their outrage duty. Now, some people are outraged all the time. It must be exhausting but the rest of us leave them to it: we have tourists to encourage and a laid-back reputation to protect. But soon enough, it will be our turn to have our really big public melt-down.

The trick with outrage is to let something get under your skin and really gnaw at you until you have no choice but to publicly erupt and let whoever's annoying you have it.

One result of constant giving out is that it's in danger of becoming a low background hum. With a history as dark and complex as The Shushening, there's very little misery that's new to us.

But don't think that familiarity will stop us exploding when we feel like getting the maximum benefit from a complaint. No, no: we know just how to milk it. And don't doubt certain people's capacity for invention when they're bored and in need of a little *faux*-outrage.

Out(rage) of all proportion for when we've too much time on our hands:

1. Same-sex relationships.

2. What's in the water?

3. The traffic.

4. The tolls.

5. The removal or addition of an ingredient to a traditional recipe.

6. How do they get the figs into the fig rolls?

7. Dogs. In general.

8. Whatever happened to the cast of *Glenroe*?

9. The weight of schoolbags.

10. Crisps used to be 4p.

11. Getting stuck behind a tractor.

12. What's the deal with yer man in that ad?

13. The 'wrong' kind of teabags.

Some of us do this as a hobby instead of the gym. We get worked up instead of working out.

Not all outrage is *faux*-outrage, of course. We have a lot to be very, very angry about. For reals. But we're still grateful for the team of bored legends who will go on the radio or take to the papers every single day to be outraged to amuse the rest of us. Thank you. It allows the rest of us to remain calm and keep really bad stuff at that low background level for fear we'd be at boiling point all the time. To those who are about to erupt on our behalf: we salute you.

Moan factor: 10/10

Optimism Optional

★ You can choose to be happy, but is that wise? ★

Putting our blinkers on nice and tight is about as close as Irish people get to optimism. Maybe we knew unbridled joy before The Shushening, but now we live in fear someone will take it away. We can't trust it. If someone is happy or positive for more than a nano-second and it isn't their birthday, it's best to take them down. It's for their own good.

Never let your own hopes get too high, because when they're dashed, you'll be miserable. This is Irish common sense, borne out by experience. Cutting a cheery person down is a kindness: you're easing them into inevitable despair and saving them an awful fright down the line. That's very nice of you.

If they're irrepressible and still don't get the message, turn it into an even more creative moaning opportunity. Go harsher. 'They think they're great'. 'They're far too up themselves'. 'They'll be sorry, wait and see'. It will reach them telepathically and they won't be long plummeting to earth. Not so foolishly optimistic now. But much safer.

Of course, the new way to cut someone down to size is anonymously, online. There's nothing Ciarán hates more than a happy Tweeter.

Let's eavesdrop on a little exchange he had with Scamall just last week.

Moan factor: 10/10

Ciarán (a.k.a. Slyfox99) vs Scamall on Twitter:

Slyfox99: Oh, Christ, the fecking liberal monkeys are at it again, saying racism is bad

Scamall: Erm . . . hello? The 21st century called. It said racism *is* bad.

Slyfox99: Racism is bad, but when you push it down my throat, you just make me want to go out and be a big racist.

Scamall: I'm not pushing anything down your throat. You should be so lucky.

Slyfox99: Oh, very mature.

Scamall: I'm immature? You posted racist epithets on iamnotanirishracist.ie

Slyfox99: Yeah. To wake you liberal parrots up. Make you think about the platitudes you squawk.

Scamall: I thought we were monkeys before. Someone's swallowed a thesaurus.

Slyfox99: You probably had to look that up. Hippie.

Scamall: That's a compliment. Thank you, anonymous coward.

Slyfox99: I'm not a coward.

Scamall: Yeah, you are. You subtweet so much you must need a periscope.

******** Ten minutes later********

Scamall: I'll take your lack of response as an admission of guilt.

Slyfox99: No, I was unpacking dinner. I do have a life off of here. Unlike you.

Scamall: Kindly address my assertion. You're a no-spine subtweeter.

Slyfox99: *facepalm* I don't tweet losers directly because I'm so SO bored of them. *doublefacepalm* *tongue out emoji*

Scamall: You don't even believe what you're saying.

Slyfox99: Waah, waaah, someone needs a waahmbulance. A liberal wambulance where everyone's nice to each other, like dicks.

*You are blocked from following @Scamall and viewing @Scamall's tweets. Learn more.

Slyfox99: Oh, look. I got blocked by whiny, no-action hippie @Scamall

****

Slyfox99: I forgot I blocked everyone.

Irish Oral

★ Not putting a tooth in it ★

Overseas, there's a general perception that Irish and British people have terrible teeth. But that's not true. We've had orthodontists for years now and local dentists can do all kinds of fancy stuff. Even if they didn't, though, when the Celtic Tiger arrived, we all became mouth-obsessed. There were teeth-whitening places on every corner and we even started brushing our tongues.

BUT THE PRICE. It's so expensive to get even basic dental work here that only the wealthiest natives and visiting diplomats can get fillings. Cosmetic stuff? Maybe the Queen (see *The Queen*) had some veneers done when she visited, but other than that, you have to leave Ireland. People go on teeth holidays (dental tourism, if you're posh) to Eastern Europe and still come back with change including the cost of travel. Some people say you might only come back with half a jaw, but, you know, so long as the teeth are alright . . .

Holding our mouths to ransom like this causes everyone to give out at one point or another – and if the giving-out is exacerbated by an unattended-to toothache, watch out. They call Jer and try to speak, but you can tell they have an ice-pack taped to their jaw, melting by the second with the rage. The *rage*.

So what if you can't afford dentistry? What if you don't even have the fare to Budapest? What if those awful radio ads for the Budapest all-in trip have made you pull at least one of your own teeth out in despair?

* Have all your teeth pulled out as soon as they come in. It worked in the seventies, why not now?

* Blacksmiths have great pulling devices. Suss out your local smithy.

* Pitch a reality show called *I Don't Believe They Have Great Orthodontists in America* and offer to be very hands-on with the research.

* Become a politician. You'll need to beam from the posters. Let us all pay for it.

* Get to know your local vet.

* Buy a great blender. It's soup for you!

* In fact, why not capitalise on the downturn by converting your nearest shut-down whitening place into a smoothie shop?

* Just don't smile. This is Ireland, you won't be expected to, anyway.

Moan factor: 2.30/ 10

P is for . . .

Potholes

★ Our neverending story ★

This is never, ever, ever, ever, ever, ever going to go away. Ever. Never. (Never. Got that?)

MADE-UP FACT

A certain quota of Irish potholes is left unfilled each year, just so we can complain about them.

Potholes are one of those subjects that elicit outrage. Not the enjoyable *faux*-kind either. In terms of seriousness, potholes may not be heroin or Ebola or who covered-up-what-in-which-diocese (clue: it wasn't the holes in the road), but they cause about as much conversational grief as any of these.

Ride a bike into a pothole, and you'll soon know about it. Bikes have been ruined by relatively small potholes and whole cyclists have vanished into larger ones, never to be seen again.

So here's the science, or whatevs. Our soft soil and softer, wetter air seem simply to melt the road surfaces away. Basically, it looks as if the county councils use icing instead of tar. But whatever it is, they don't seem to have enough of it. They try – slowly, so slowly – to fill in the potholes but by the (very slow) time they've patched one up, another cyclist or pedestrian has disappeared into another. Potholes simply can't or won't stay fixed.

So they're with us to stay. Turn this to your giving-out advantage: if you run out of anything else to moan about (YOU WON'T), potholes are the default fallback.

Here are some angles to get you started:

* You could moan about road safety and cyclist disappearance.

* It could be the slow – so slow – methodical work of the county council folk that you feel

you could do quicker with some Polyfilla and a trowel. Or a piping bag.

* Maybe you think they should be chlorinated and used as swimming-pools.

* Maybe you feel there aren't enough near you, and you give out about being left out of the national conversation.

It doesn't matter: you'll find something about potholes to enrage you. In many ways, potholes are your giving-out home.

Moan factor: 10/10

Tom in his cab:

'Seemingly there are so many potholes in the country, at least 3.75 people in any given county are talking about them at any given time. At any given time! That's shockin'. But will the government listen? Will they f— Talking out of their own potholes, they are.'

Pneumonyeah!

★ InVESTing in health insurance ★

You may be surprised to hear that every single person on the island of Ireland has had pneumonia, or been *this close*. Yeah, we know it's not medically possible, but we *have*.

We don't get common colds here. Ever. Amazing, given our moist, mild winters. They should be focusing global-cure research on us. We get cold symptoms, all right, and what you might think looks like a cold, but we never get 'just a cold'. Even a 'bad cold'. What we get is much, much worse.

Irish Grandmothers Or Grannies (iGOGs) know everything. We learn our approach to illness from them. Older iGOGs grew up in pre-vaccination days when everyone died from everything. The first sign of a sniffle was pronounced TB just in case and you were whisked off to a sanatorium, where you were expected to either get better or write amazing poems about your tragic decline. 'So young,' they would say, weeping over pages of your beautiful words with a precautionary hanky over their mouth and nose.

Kidney infections were caught from cold steps, where kidney infectors apparently hung out, waiting to invade your kidneys via the bum of your jeans. You were not to argue the medical improbability of this, or you'd soon be diagnosed with a thick ear, or a wooden spoon to the back of the legs. (Actually, this was the only thing to which the jeans could actually make you immune.)

But when it came to pneumonia, there was a sure-fire way to get it – NO QUESTION, NO DOUBT – *go out without a vest on you.*

There seems to have been an agreement in this country that illnesses got in through most other clothing (see useless jeans above), but germs were halted at the thorax if you had this specific suit of cotton armour over it, i.e. the vest. Presumably, airborne bugs could only get so high – never rising above the height of a child's chest – or you'd have had to wear the precautionary hanky over the mouth and nose at all times from September to May. But it seems that, mainly, bugs concentrated on the chest area, and a simple cotton singlet was enough to see them all off.

We may give out about healthcare, but illness is one of the things we don't moan too much about here. It's too serious to find entertaining. And we're traditionally used to the slightest thing carrying someone off, which nobody wants, no matter how good the death. So it's great you can stave it off with something you can get three-for-a-tenner in practically any department store.

If you think health insurance is a relatively new idea, you don't know about the Irish relationship with vests. There was also a premium policy: if an iGOG pinned a scapular to that vest, you were golden even into the next life. So even if the bugs made it past the cotton and you were carried off, you'd be grand.

Moan factor: TB/10

Tom in his cab:

'I hate having sick people in me cab. I hate it, I do. If someone calls me late at night and they sound a bit peakish, good night! I'm not taking them. You could get all sorts in the back – spew, the lot. And even if there's nothing coming out of them, I don't want to risk getting it meself. I work for me and me boss is a bollix. Ha!'

Price of a Pint

★ The worst and most shocking disgrace of them all ★

High Drama alert! Pints all over Ireland are too expensive and it's a shocking disgrace and we all give out loudly about it – even as we wipe the creamy foam of the second one of the evening from our no-longer-parched top lips.

Pints aren't just pints, you see: pints reflect the cost of *really* living. If you can't afford a few pints, what's the point of all that hard work and taxpaying in the first place?

'Pints' might mean wine or coffee or cool sparkling water, but pints in the local have been the cornerstone of our social lives and highlight of our week for centuries. A necessity, not a luxury.

Especially after The Shushening, when we got a little

strange around each other, pints brought us together and helped us un-squish. Moreover, meeting on neutral ground means you can always leave if someone's annoying the arse off you so long as you've paid your way in the round. Which you can only do if you can afford it.

Which brings us back to the price.

Irish people are always in shock when we come back from a trip to anywhere-but-Sweden bringing tales of how little it costs to live elsewhere (except Sweden). We're not talking the weekly grocery shop or education or health insurance – we'll have used our time away to pretend these don't exist, and that we look good in shorts – but we will all have been for a pint. We may not speak the language and the currency might baffle us, but we will have learned how to say, 'Two beers', and whether or not we've been given the wrong change, just by the weight of it in our sunburned hands.

We are passionate about many things – sport, politics, literature – but where are we going to sort them out? Over a pint, that's where.

On social media, if there are no pics, it didn't happen. Well, here it hasn't really happened till it's been discussed over a pint or three in the local.

Imagine if we couldn't afford it? Sure, the country would fall apart.

Máiréad believes the price of alcohol should be raised for people's own good:

'No one can argue that alcohol abuse is a huge problem in this country, but I think it's time we hit people where it hurts. In the pocket, that is. People's pockets seem only stuffed with drinking money.

I can't go around to every pub, telling people to stop when I think they've had enough. I tried that, but I was barred for "annoying people". Really. It just shows how times have changed and that there's no respect. For me.

'I know you were talking to that lady before, Jer, who said it'd be like Prohibition and people would all be driven underground to speakeasies offering cheap hooch and the like. But that's highly unlikely. There aren't even that many basements in Ireland.

'I'd also like to come back to what she said about people on lower incomes sacrificing food or bills, sitting in the dark just to be able to afford their scoops and all the rest of it. But I wouldn't do that, and if I wouldn't do it, it's definitely not going to happen.

'So raise those prices high. That's the kind of Ireland I want to live in.'

This nanny-style, price-raising proposition could be a real

powder keg. Which might soon be the only kind of keg we can afford.

Moan factor: 9/10

Poping the Question

★ Vatican or Vatican't? ★

We're very conflicted about the Vatican here now. But Ireland used to be a place where a pope was welcomed by a million open arms. For a certain generation, there is only one pope and that's John Paul II. He came to Ireland in 1979 and everyone got the day off school to watch him say mass on telly. Who doesn't love a day off? So, for a while, everyone loved the Pope.

Well, maybe not everyone. There were lots of people who had the feeling that he wasn't all he was cracked up to be, day off or no day off. But their voices were sort of drowned out with all the charismatic singing and they had to keep giving out underground, like some kind of anti-Vatican resistance movement, knowing that one day The Shushening would be over and the people who weren't pope fans would have their chance to give out.

But in 1979, that day seemed very far off. Probably almost as many people went on the bus to see him as went to the Moving Statues, so he was still very important. The country went nuts. Nuts 'great' or nuts 'white with rage' depended very much on whether you were a papal fan or not.

Papal visit pros	Papal visit cons
✳ Dana, Ireland's most musical virginal future presidential candidate, ditched her attempt at a sexy comeback (no, really) and released a holy single for the pope.	✳ It was like punk never happened.
✳ Everyone bought a medal with his face on it.	✳ Just when you thought medallions were on the way out.
✳ Religious higher-ups ran around with massive erections ('He's here! He's here!').	✳ The erections were nothing new. But still. Ew.
✳ We got a day off!	✳ To watch a mass. Not even in hi-def.
✳ JOBS!	✳ We can't argue with that one.

* The young people of the country were, for a moment, united in peace.

* He laid hands on old folks and there were many reported healings.

* Priests had a second career as holy warm-up men. (Make that third: we've already mentioned that some of them were pretty great dads.)

* Some of the kids were the priests' own. But let's not dwell on that.

* Some of those old folks were practically hurled at JP for blessings.

* Some of them only wanted to go to the bingo and thought that was where the coach was heading.

If 'mass Rocks' is the slogan the Irish clergy should have had, then this was the stadium tour. Popeapalooza. It's probably what inspired U2.

A lot has changed since 1979: Magdalene laundries were still going then. (Who do you think washed the papal undies? The nuns were too busy licking his feet.) There was no divorce yet and no Gays. The pope really had us in his pocket but, then, these were much more innocent times, if you were willing to ignore the kids vs clergy thing. And a lot of people were. But I guess holy medals can be a bit blinding.

But you have to understand that, back then, we loved who we were told to by the telly. We only had the one channel, so that was basically Gay Byrne, Bosco and All-Ireland hurling finalists.

So when a cute lookin' oul' fella with a hot accent got us a day off and told us, 'I luff you,' *on telly*, no wonder it turned our heads.

Moan factor: II (that's 2, not 11)/10

Pants on Fire

★ We're lying if we say we don't love liars ★

We love a good story and a good storyteller is prized and admired. Even a bad one will do. So, lying holds a complex place in our society.

We might say we value truth and integrity above all else, but that's a little white lie. We secretly seem to appreciate being duped, so long as the duping process itself has been enjoyable. When it hasn't, the bolder and more flamboyant the lie, the more likely we are to let the liar back into the fold to keep lying, with a few slaps on the back, as if to say, 'Jez, they were good lies, now, fair play to ya.'

Lies like 'You're all rich!' are gobbled up like they

were brunch, even though we know in our hearts that we should never have been asked to try and carry brunch off. If a storyteller – or, to give them their more basic name, 'liar' – weaves a verbal tapestry, we're mesmerised. We give that person a crown. And when the lie is eventually revealed we say we never knew. Oh, we're so shocked!

But, really, we *did* know. We were just enjoying the ride – even the downhill part.

Moan factor: 5 (or is it?)/10

Q is for . . .

The Queen

★ One is finally amused ★

Ah, no, Yer Maj! It was all going so well and then out came the footage of the old Nazi salute. Never mind: of all people, Irish people will be able to overlook it. There's a ton of stuff we did during 'The Emergency' (WWII) that we'd rather not talk about now. Oh, look! Bunting!

Decades after that papal visit, Ireland had another significant visitor: Queen Elizabeth II of England, a.k.a. 'The Queen'. It sounds a bit like an East End gangster nickname, but from what we can ascertain, she's legit.

Time was, if you went to England to work and take

'the Queen's shilling', you became 'Johnny Turncoat'. As far as everyone at home was concerned, you might as well have taken a big old steaming bowl of soup during the Famine, done a review of it in the local paper, given it five stars and renounced your Irish roots while you were at it.

The Good Friday Agreement made things a lot better between Ireland and Britain – the pre-Twitter Taylor Swift vs Nicki Minaj – and even though we don't give out about Britain any more, there was still a bit of residual sneering. If your auntie picked up *Hello!* magazine to check out photos of the new royal baby or some duchess's wedding, she became a pariah. She was Jilly Turncoat, even though the only thing she'd turned were the pages of a crappy magazine she found in the doctor's surgery.

It was not cool to be into the royals. If you took pictures of Buckingham Palace while on holiday, you'd be doomed to show them only in underground caverns to a select group. (NB: A very different underground gang from the Vatican't.) If a royal died or got married or had an affair, you had to pretend you hadn't heard about it – even though it was the best soap opera ever.

Then, all of a sudden, the Queen came. Here. She didn't only come to Northern Ireland, no: she came to see us, in the Republic, where we don't care about kings or queens at all, at all. For a moment, we wondered if anyone would be there to meet her or if she'd be given her tea. Well, blow us if we didn't get all giddy and dizzy and go a-hunting out our best petticoats or anything else we could wave at her in the streets:

And blow us further if she didn't charm the petticoats right off us. She smiled. She waved. She bowed her head at the right monuments.

And, best of all, she gave us a *wonderful* opportunity for giving out.

* How many taxpayers euros were going on her security detail?

* Why was a republic getting so het up about the visit of a monarch – the monarch of a country that used to shushen the shite out of us?

* Weren't her great-great-whatever-the-whats only bastards, and here were we, giving her her dinner in Dublin Castle? Michael Collins would be turning in his grave.

* No, you shut up! 'She's just a little old lady now', me eye!

* Is that Irish she's trying to speak? Pfft. I mean, it's not bad, and it's a nice gesture, but she obviously doesn't know the first thing about the *tiseal ginideach*.

It was a PR coup – the only kind of coup royals are really down with. By the time she had her smiliest ever photo taken with a Cork butcher, the country had properly invoked the 'your nan' clause. Now, every time someone says, 'Eight hundred years of oppression', you can be sure some bright spark will have a sup of a pint and say, 'Ah, but didn't the Queen have the time of her life in Cork?'

Moan factor: ERII/10

R is for . . .

Racist

★ (Not being, but . . .) ★

As we saw earlier in *Black Fellas*, no one in Ireland is racist, which is brilliant. In fact, we're so not racist, it's worth another look here.

To show quite how not racist we are, we give migrants and asylum-seekers camps to stay in. Camping! Just like our own homeless. So you see, really, we're treating them no different. We give these camps a lovely name: 'Direct Provision', *providing* (very little) aid *directly* to these newly arrived families. Like a big, cruel sleepover, everyone (kids and adults, all ages) crams in together! Who knows who sees what? Isn't that great preparation for the adult world? The next fun challenge is to make €19.10 last a whole week – so much better than your regular low-stakes scavenger hunt. This is good training for if ever the person is allowed to join the workforce. Eventually. Ever. Meanwhile, everyone gets to eat junk food, paid for by the state. The state doesn't buy me any junk food. Doesn't it sound like fun?

We can only hope that, some day, the people currently in Direct Provision will forgive us. Then we'll all look back and laugh *together* – just like we do about things like systemic abuse in the Church, and other stuff that didn't happen either.

Here are some of the cool things we'll say:

* It was a different time.

* We didn't know any better.

* I'm not racist but, as a mother, I was worried that my own kids would be affected somehow.

* Sure, we're hardly able to look after ourselves, big eejits that we are. The joke's on us!

* Only in Ireland!

Ha-ha! Ah.

If nothing else, this misery will set up these new

arrivals – just like the rest of us – to be absolute experts at giving out.

Moan factor: 8.5/10

Referendumb

★ Our constitutional fear of change ★

In 2015, we had our big and brilliant Marriage Equality Referendum. (Actually, there was another referendum on the day but we can't remember what for now. Nobody really mentioned it at the time.) Whether you were for or against, everyone was very excited about it. This was a surprise, because Irish people are usually very apathetic about voting.

But when you look at it, a referendum is just a great big excuse to give out. Yes or No? You're either one or the other and you can give out about the 'other side' for months. You can even make things up about them, for 'Balance'!

Whether you agree with all it contains or not, we Irish love our constitution. It only leaves out the fundamental rights of a few of us now, so what's not to love? Sure, the original was so holy, it was sent to the pope for the old once-over before it was even shown to the people. We mean, *really* holy, which is one of the main reasons that everyone in Ireland is Catholic – even those of us who aren't. But times have changed. Whatever our religious beliefs, one day we might even get to give the constitution a makeover, saying we'd prefer the state didn't make decisions for individuals any more, like what they put into their tea, or wombs.

But for now, we can just give out about the bits of the constitution that leave us out. Don't worry, the government won't do anything about it. We know they'll come up with a different silly referendum with a particularly confusingly worded yes/no question to distract us for a while, like, 'Should all women in the Seanad not be called Cáit?' or 'Should the height of a president not be over five foot?' And then we can give out about that.

Nothing like a referendum to clean out government coffers so they can say, 'Oh, I agree with you. All presidents should be giants, but we just don't have the money for another referendum right now.' But when the options are a Yes or No answer, surely a few pencils and bits of paper can sort it? It's frustrating referenda cost so much when we could sort a lot of this crap out in the local or online. We'd almost definitely give out more – in a more proactive way – if referenda made us feel that we, the people, really had a say. Instead, they make us feel like we're part of an exciting, dynamic and evolving democracy, one in which we'll be heard. (Unless you're a woman. But more about the pesky Vagina Owners later.) They're really distracting us from the fact that we're not, really. So, instead of taking to the ballot box, we take to the airwaves.

But is that true? Answer Yes or No on a ballot paper.

Moan factor: 5/10

Seán on the Marriage Equality Referendum campaign:

'I was going to vote No in the gay-marriage thing because I can't cook and it'd be terrible if there were two of us in the house that couldn't. Sure, the place would fall apart. So I'd hate that to happen to anyone else, and young people don't be thinking ahead like that. And the priest had said that the old gay sex thing wasn't God's bag. I'd heard that before but, to be honest, I never paid it much mind because, as far as I'm concerned, God doesn't be looking at you all the time. He's off doing miracles. And if He didn't like gay fellas or gay young wans, wouldn't He have miracled them not be gay? But He didn't. So there you are. I still won't be telling anyone how I voted, though.'

Theory of Relativity

★ Giving out about family ★

In fairness to them, the dead and/or distant relatives we met in *Kin-sternation* are the least of our worries. It's the living ones that give us real cause for giving out.

Everyone everywhere complains about their family (see *iMOM* for mammy protocol, though), but in Ireland we have more of them in closer proximity, so when it comes to giving out, we've had a lot of practice.

We're not sure why the Kin are so hot on being related: to Irish people, it's very, very stressful. An Irish family either wants to see you all the time or pretend you don't exist. Somehow neither ever coincides with how you feel about them: if you want a bit of privacy, guaranteed there'll be an enormous funeral of a third cousin you've never met that you have to attend on pain of banishment.

If, on the other hand, you actually fancy a bit of family time, you may find you're already in a period of banishment for something you don't even remember but they *all* do.

It can't be avoided. Families are huge. As mentioned earlier, we only got contraception about two years ago and only realised we probably weren't going to Hell for using it sometime around last week, so there are only *loads* of Irish relatives. Practically everyone is your cousin. Put aside how icky this sounds if you're looking for the ride on the island (basically, CHOOSE THOSE ONE-NIGHT STANDS WITH CARE) and you actually get a pretty sweet concept.

In Ireland, you're either a relation or a 'connection': your cousin marries the in-laws of another cousin and now you're all double super-cousins. Surprisingly, rarely does this lead to having your wedding day ruined by an

Tara Flynn

aunt revealing that you and your new spouse are already family, and that your offspring might not win any Nobel prizes. It might be best to consult your Kin for family-tree action before actually getting engaged.

Other than that, you're usually better off not worrying who your distant relatives are (it's everyone). The ones you're close to are handful enough.

In any large group of people, a concert arena, say, there's no onus on the crowd to get on with each other: you're just some folks who love Beyoncé. You're not expected to forgive anyone for elbowing you in the face. You can forget them as soon as you're on the Luas. Well, Irish families are like arenas full of people you're expected to (a) know and (b) like, no matter who elbows who in the face. It's a nightmare.

The fact is, at any one time, only about three members of any Irish family are actually in communication with each other. The others have to employ meaningful looks, carrier pigeons and espionage to get messages across.

That said, we will happily talk to Jer all day about some family feud or other, privacy be damned.

An Irish family is strong, stubborn and amazing to have in your corner. But, as seen in *iMOM*, if you're ever asked to join in on giving out about anyone else's relatives, your best bet is to stuff your face with cake and nod. Cake is your only refuge here.

Moan factor: 10/10

Scamall on family:

'I haven't seen most of my family in five years. I see my dad sometimes, when I need fuel for the car or I've had a bad day's foraging and I need chips. Or money. I get him to do my chips for me in fresh oil so I don't take on any negative chipper energy. My dad's okay.

'My mother was the kind who didn't want any "creatives" in the house. And that's just who I am. I can't change my creative soul. "It's just such an insecure life," my mother would say. "Besides, there are enough paintings now, aren't there? We wouldn't want the world to run out of frames."

'I had to cut myself off from that kind of uptight energy before it totally creased my inner ironing.'

Rung Up

★ Ladders ★

There are four types of ladder you can give out about in Ireland:

1. Actual ladders: These may get you up onto the roof (which you need, after a storm) but they are very dangerous. They can slip, or fall on you or . . .

2. . . . you might walk under one, which is bad luck. A superstitious nation, it's a wonder more people don't get sued for leaving them against the wall on their lunchbreak.

3. Ladders in your tights: It's cold. Even in summer. Unless you're wearing trousers (sometimes even when you're wearing them) you'll have to wear tights. You too, lads. No shame in it. However, tights ladder the very first time you put them on. If not before. They are just awful.

4. The property ladder: This term has practically led to the banning of both the words 'property' and 'ladder' from Hiberno-English. You were supposed to get on this as quickly as possible and climb up it as high as you could. So people did. And they slipped. Or one fell on us. Which is, as we know, just what ladders do. And no one was there to hold it steady. With property prices going up and down like yo-yos, there was really no safe ground for a ladder at all.

And then, they kicked us in the eye.

Moan factor: 5/10

Roboconductors™

How to keep rowdy rail passengers – like leaves – on track

Mentioned briefly in 'Getting Around the island 2: Trains', we're back to solve some of the issues of the Irish rail system. Hopefully not at the expense of some A-grade giving out, though.

The Irish train-travel experience is indescribable; you really just have to live it. Even if you get from A to B on time through stunning countryside, you'll find something to give out about, we know you will. We have faith in you.

Like that time you got stuck behind the refreshments trolley and had to inch through each carriage for the entire journey and you were so apoplectic that you nearly had a stroke on the way back from the buffet car. You did still get where you were going on time. And there was great Wi-Fi, so you were able to tweet your displeasure straight to the company. So it's really not so bad.

Especially now: it used to be that if you missed the Cork train, you missed Christmas. Now there'll be another one along in an hour.

But luckily for givers-out, Irish trains still aren't as frequent as those in other countries and you might end up sitting by the loo all the way to Galway on a busy weekend. Or someone might be sitting in your pre-booked seat, toughing it out, pretending to be you, shoving an ID card in your face that they clearly just made out of the magazine they found under the seat. *Your* seat. There's no one there to sort it out except the lovely trolley lady, who, when she took the job, wanted nothing more than to make crappy coffee in paper cups and see Ireland in peace. Now she sees passengers about to come to blows and there she is, Taserless, between a trolley and a hard place. There's no amount of pre-packaged ham-and-cheese sandwiches she can throw at the situation to defuse it.

If things really escalate, the trolley person has to alert the driver, who has to stop the train at a station and call the guards. Since local station closures in the sixties, it could be hours till the next one – months, if there are 'leaves on the track' – and you might already be dead by then. The person pretending to be you could, by that stage, have poisoned your coffee and fully assumed your identity. Or, in a particularly poorly served part of the country, old age might eventually have got the lot of you.

We'd like to propose something that could make the journey near-perfect: not just twenty-first century standard but twenty-first century Japan standard. So often, the main reason for giving out about a train journey is the absence of conductors on some services. Conductors who could defuse and deal with a situation, say, where someone were to impersonate a nice, normal person who'd booked online and used a hilarious pretend name to pre-book their seat. Conductors who could take charge, as well as our tickets. Conductors who could punch not just those tickets but your lights out.

Our twenty-first century solution: Roboconductors™.

For when you don't have enough staff or they just don't turn up at weekends, Roboconductors™ will replace human workers.

Roboconductors™ are big and strong and have Tasers for fingers, but are not wide enough to block the aisle. You could have a Roboconductor™ in every carriage on match days.

Roboconductors™ could be programmed to reprimand people for the following:

* Putting feet on seats.

* Not understanding the announcements in Irish (they will correct grammar upon detecting it being spoken badly).

* Loud singing of terrible or terribly offensive songs.

* Opening smelly food near other humans.

* Impersonating another passenger – who's clearly booked their seat online – using a crude ID card fashioned from a magazine.

If these changes were implemented, the only downside would be that we'd have nothing to give out about on trains. On the upside robots!

Moan factor: 6/10 (9/10 on match days)

$ is for . . .

Sneaks

★ Lowest of the low ★

Being sneaky in Ireland is to attract a fate worse than death. If someone finds out you've been sneaky, you will be openly given out about and condemned up and down the land. See? Much worse than death. Death sounds cosy and inviting compared to being a sneak. Nothing sneaky about this giving out, either: rest assured, it will be in your face. A kind of medieval-style shunning, if you will. They'll have to shun you, too, because they're already using the stocks on blaspheming comedians.

If we're honest, Irish people are fairly comfortable with our two-faced nature:

> **Seán:** 'No, Jim, I don't want a pint!' *Jim goes to the bar.*
> 'Jesus, Jim never bought me a pint.'

Jim should have known better than to go to the bar and

come back empty-handed. Never, ever believe someone doesn't want to be bought something.

There's a difference between being 'sneaky' and being 'cute'.

Two-facedness in the 'cute' sense has a time and a place. We're fairly empathetic, often pretending to agree with someone in order to minimise their discomfort. We want you to think we're lovely, so we'll hardly ever let you know if we think you're not. After all, we need you to keep coming back to our pub/restaurant/radio show/ from the bar not empty-handed.

Sneakiness, though, earns you universal disdain. Here's what sneaky looks like:

* Winning the lotto and not telling your neighbours, let alone volunteering half your haul to get the potholes on the cul-de-sac fixed.

* Committing a 'bad' crime – like stealing an art collection or buying some pills online. Not rape, though. Rape seems to be okay.

* Giving out a 100 per cent mortgage in 2004 and crying that you never knew no one could pay it back by 2008.

* Pretending women only go to England for the craic.

* Selling off an airline when people live on an island.

* Charging people for domestic water . . . in advance of knowing the cost.

A little bit of two-facedness is there to protect us all and keep us from killing each other. Being sneaky is one-sided – only there for personal gain.

And if you do ever choose to do something sneaky, FOR THE LOVE OF GOD do a great job covering it up. Or move. Those are your options.

Moan factor: 9/10

Soccer

★ Olé Olé O-look, we didn't give out for a minute ★

We're not going to get into who-accepted-€5-million-for-what, or who-hand-balled-who-out-of-a-chance-at-the-World-Cup. There's a whole other book in that. In fact, it's probably number one in the charts this week, so we're very glad you picked this one up at all.

We're going to look at soccer in a more general givey-outy way.

We'd have put this under F, for 'Football' but (a) we realised we were giving out about loads of Fs and (b) we want to make the distinction between 'Gaelic Football', about which nobody moans unless their county is losing, and 'Football Football'. The English kind. Soccer.

For ages, we weren't supposed to like it because of England. But, as we know, that's all okay now.

It was easy not to like it in and of itself, mind you, given that we generally weren't very good at it. Down south, we couldn't even claim George Best, even though we desperately wanted to.

Many young people grew up supporting a British team, referring to losses and gains with the 'we' word: '*We* lost.' Or '*We* won.' Even though they'd never been to a match and were now supposedly going to be banned from St Patrick's Day for even thinking such soccery thoughts.

But then, in 1990, everything changed.

We only went and got hope. And it was as terrible as we'd always feared. (See *Optimism Optional*.)

In 1990, the Republic of Ireland football team got through to the World Cup finals, or Italia '90 as it was called. The country had never known pride like it. In fact, although lots of other things happened in 1990, no one who was in Ireland at the time remembers them. We don't even want to.

People who'd never watched football before were getting time off work to watch matches in pubs. Employers shut up businesses for the day – unless they owned pubs. The country went football crazy, football mad and every eleven-year-old named John Paul sang, 'We're all part of

Jackie's Army!' threateningly from the top deck of every bus. Fellas went off to Italy with only green clothes in their suitcases, and became the best and nicest soccer fans anywhere, ever.

Back home, bunting seemed to be holding houses up, even in the most previously anti-soccer homes. Everyone smiled at each other. It was as if Ireland held its breath, and for the length of that breath there was no giving out. It was a hell of a summer, with 'hell' turning out to be the operative word.

Because, as most Irish dreams, Italia '90 was to end, abruptly, overseas. Italy beat the crap out of us, putting us out of the tournament and back in our place. Our Lads gave TV interviews about being sick as parrots and feeling like they'd let the fans down. Which they had. In fact, they'd broken our hearts and killed the very concept of hope itself. But we'd never let them know it. They were Jackie's Army. Our army. They'd given it their best shot and we loved them for it.

However, unlike grudges, we have short memories where hope is concerned. So we try to keep up our liking for soccer, but we do end up having to give out about it. Every four years, we let the World Cup tease us again. 'Ireland could win it this time! Or just be in it! We could be happy! Thierry who? We should have five million reasons to hate this, but WE LOVE IT. Remember Italia '90? That happened, right?'

It did. But it probably shouldn't have. Singing *Ireland are the greatest . . .* anything is dangerous. Roy Keane could fly home at any point, the best in the world at giving out, if not at staying put. Getting our hopes up isn't the national pastime for a reason: we know how it ends.

But still we put on our jerseys and cheer to hoarseness, especially when the Boys aren't looking so good. That's when we really come into our own, when our history of Shushening brings out the best in us. If things on the pitch get really bad, when other countries might give up and give out, we sing 'The Fields of Athenry' (an uplifting song about hunger and deportation) to make us all feel better. It doesn't, but at least we get a singsong in.

Soccer giveth and soccer taketh away, but it definitely giveth us plenty to give out about. And it shows us that, sometimes, the best way to give out is to sing about it.

But sing it quietly; don't commit. Not fully. You'll only have the heart torn out of yourself.

Moan factor: 1–0/10

Tom in his cab tells Jer about how he remembers Italia '90:

'Ah, it was terrible, Jer. Awful, now. Sure wasn't it sunny the whole time, and that's terrible for taxis. You'd swear we didn't exist till the next spit of rain. Anyway, the streets were empty, so they were.

Everyone was inside with the telly – apart from the few bright sparks who stayed home with the cans and took the telly outside. You don't need a cab to go from the fridge to the garden so we lost out there, too.

'I gave in, Jer. I parked my cab up. There was no point. But once I got to the pub, I was fuming. Packed, it was. How did everyone get there? There was no one on the streets – they must have had to go from the house to the pub somehow, y'know? Maybe there were underground tunnels or something. Especially on the southside. You wouldn't know what they'd be up to.

'Anyway, however they did it, people got to the pubs, with no fares for me. A disaster, so it was. A disaster. I take your point, Jer, that the country had a great party, but it wasn't till we got the boot that I got fares again. That was a great day for Ireland, as far as I'm concerned.'

Social Meeja

★ Tweeting our Face(book)s off ★

If you were to believe certain commentators, in the few short years since its inception social media has ruined the country entirely. Incredible. Ireland has withstood famine, persecution, mass emigration, civil and world wars, but who knew that we could be brought to our knees by 140 characters and a few old hashtags?

Despite the inevitable few bored trolls out for sport (we're not looking at you, Ciarán), social media has been a positive force in and for Ireland. So much of what kept The Shushening in place was shame and isolation: 'I'm bad, and I'll be shunned like a sneak for my badness.' What social media did was to show us that we weren't alone.

Before the internet, many of us wanted change. We just didn't know it was possible. Those standing to benefit from The Shushening spouted unchallenged sermons about how change was bad and we had no option but to accept. We instinctively felt certain things were unfair but had no one to bounce them off. Then (*fanfare*), the internet arrived.

Finally, we were able to connect with like-minded people online. Loads of them – loads of them even in Ireland. Ideas spread like wildfire. Forums filled with 'I don't like this . . .' and 'I agree!'

Ten years ago, nobody even attempted to broach less popular topics like *Aborshhh* . . . or baseball or a fascination for feet, because they felt they were the only ones. But since social media helped to bring them together more and more people can say 'baseball' without fear of derision or shouts of, 'Go on home to New Jersey.' They've found other baseball supporters online. Some even get to play in real life (IRL). We're not sure about the feet guys, but we hope they get to play, too.

But, of course, there's a flipside. Online anonymity leads to just as many trolling shenanigans in Irish social media as in a Norwegian folk tale. And because we're all experts at giving out, their trolling skillz are unparalleled. Tedious, but unparalleled.

Those not caught up with Ireland's lightning-fast change can lash out anonymously online. (NB: Just because your avatar is a My Little Pony, not everyone thinks you're cute: it doesn't give you a free pass to be mean.) This kind of thing teeters dangerously towards the sneaky. (See *Sneaks*)

Mind you, some of the best giving-out entertainment comes from these brave online vigilantes, who wouldn't want their voices recognised on the radio. These people almost certainly never give out IRL – they just take to their keyboards to do so and, boy, do they let rip. The My Little Ponys we remember never swore like that.

Moan factor: 8/10

Space: The Final Frontier

★ Crowded housing ★

By buying way too many properties – each – in the early noughties, we somehow made overcrowding from nothing.

Even though the Famine and emigration did their space-clearing thing, somehow there still aren't enough places to live. Especially if you don't have a job. Or you're newly arrived from a war-torn country. Or you believed the bank when they said you'd be able to repay them, the scamps. Or maybe you just prefer living in the car with your two kids? Or you just really, really like camping?

In certain parts of Ireland, you can go ten miles in all directions without seeing a sheep, let alone a person, yet people still find themselves sleeping on the streets. It's amazing. Only in Ireland. Amirite?

Moan factor: 9/10

> Tom in his taxi, not getting people living in cars:
>
> 'Don't get me wrong now, Jer, I think it's terrible 'n' all. But, like, if you've a car, you have to have money. How else could you buy petrol or do the NCT? I love my car. My wife and I went on our honeymoon to Connemara and we slept in the car and it was lovely. Loved it, we did. Saved a fortune, too. Beautiful place, Connemara. Maybe that lady who rang in before with the kids in the car could move down there? It's beautiful, Jer. Beautiful, now. She could

drive it in four hours with the new roads. I'd say the kids would love it, so they would.'

Tis for . . .

Tee Party

★ You're not supposed to give out about golf ★

You can only give out about golf in a peripheral way. Especially when an amateur like Paul Dunne can crush it at the British Open, keeping the pros on their toes and giving us all hope. Dangerous, almost Italia-'90-level hope. You could maybe give out about, say, whether or not Rory McIlroy is Team Ireland or Team GB this week, and whose business is it anyway? Or whether Shane Lowry is a magician? That's actually a safer conversational zone than criticising a course or the game itself.

There is, according to several tourism sites, more golf per capita in Ireland than practically anywhere else in the world. Whether 'more golf' refers to gear owned, available acres of clubland, golfers in the family or number of courses per Irish head is unclear, but there's the fact for you: more golf per capita. It sounds sort of prosperous and successful, so let's go with it. We need the boost. Greens shoots, if you will.

Golf brings in a whole heap of tourist dollars. So much so, we've even been known to turn a blind eye when a beautiful natural area is turned into bunkers with helipads, but you can't really give out about the fact that billionaire tourists need somewhere to land. That's tourist-dollar physics right there.

The truth is, we will gleefully give out about everything in Ireland . . . unless it brings revenue into the country. Then the complaining is supposed to stop. You're a traitor if you question it. Stop hurting Ireland! So the Old Head of Kinsale is greens and fairways now, and only the very wealthy can visit it?

But think of the JOBS.

Moan factor: 18 holes/10

Tom in his cab. He really is on a roll:

'I proposed to my wife on those cliffs, where they're putting that new course. Exclusive la-di-da 'n' all. I've beautiful memories of the place, beautiful. But it's good for the country, isn't it, at the same time, at the end of the day? No, it is. Why wouldn't you want Ireland to prosper? That's a terrible attitude to have and the economy the way it is. If you've that attitude, you must be doing all right for yourself. Ah, no, I'm only messing with you. Only messing. I love the golf, though, I do. I always have the clubs in the back. Do you play? You don't?'

(Uncomfortable silence.)

And even if you feel it's the most boring game ever and couldn't they all just go for a lovely walk, take in the stunning views and talk to each other? Don't give out about it. That would be blasphemy. €25,000, please.

Tourists

★ Giving out about people we ask to come here or 'Céad Míle Fault You' ★

This section is aimed at you many lovely people who visit our shores, most of whom are lovely. The lovely ones are fine. You're lovely.

We want to try to reach the irritating few who come and give us massive cause for giving out. If, instead of doing our accent badly at us*, you choose to listen for a change, you might have a much more awesome time next time you come.

---

* Listen, we get it: our accent is hard to do. Impossible, even. But let's clear something up FOR EVER: the accent of the Lucky Charms leprechaun IS NOT AN IRISH ACCENT. We never even had that commercial. There are hundreds of local accents all around the country and that leprechaun isn't even doing one of them. He could at least have had the decency to pick one before attempting to pump kids full of sugar. So let's retire this made-up accent. At least to our faces. Please. It's for your own safety.

We have a terrible confession to make. We *love* to complain about tourists, so you only need to give us the slightest excuse. Even though we make pretty awful tourists ourselves (see 'Getting off the island: overseas travel') we have zero tolerance for people who annoy us at home, bellowing at us for directions and demanding good customer service. WTactualF?

We know, we know: 'JOBS, JOBS, the economy, tourism, what will the neighbours say? JOBS.' But no matter how much we need them, we have to admit that some tourists drive us nuts.

Bad tourists	Lovely tourists
* The bad kind of tourist step-dances out of an air-conditioned, bagpipe-music-playing coach, wearing head-to-toe Scottish tartan. They have no idea what's wrong with this picture. (If you don't either, maybe look 'Scotland' up.)	* Lovely tourists quietly cycle around, buying expensive Aran jumpers, which only tourists wear, drink the odd half-pint and get immediately hammered, attempt to join in the odd singsong and then quietly leave.

* They then act as if they're in a Disneyland theme park, instead of real, working towns where people have actual jobs and ambulances need to get by. But, no, you take your picture, it's fine. The guy in the back is only faking a stroke to make your experience more authentic!

* They walk off pavements directly into traffic, as if we drive dodgems instead of real cars.

* They think films shot on sound stages in Hollywood with no Irish people in them are historical documents. In fact, they think ads for soap and cereal are.

* They read the odd history book and ask the odd question, and are fairly clear they're not in Scotland.

* They learn how to play the tin whistle but keep it in their pockets till they're home, so as not to show us up or piss us off.

* They leave their tourist dollars and leave us alone. This could be the beginning of a beautiful friendship.

* Toora-loora-loora?
  We can tell from the
  opening bars whether
  a song has ever had the
  whiff of Ireland, or is a
  big fat phoney: the ones
  in those movies are the
  latter. Bemoaning this
  takes up a good half of
  every St Patrick's Day,
  no messing.

* They ask if they can
  help at the B&B. The
  bean an tí always says
  no, but she does like
  to be asked.

* Worst of all, they do
  'our accent'* at us,
  but really it's from a
  commercial voiced by
  someone who never
  left Boise, Idaho. Quite
  frankly, they're lucky
  they're alive.

* They speak a few
  words of Irish but
  have the good grace to
  look ashamed of the
  pronunciation.

It's our own fault and we know it: we've allowed the
traditional image of ourselves that sells so well to go on a
lot longer than it should. Celtic women bat their eyelids
and sing at American millionaires, thereby perpetuating
dangerous dancing-at-the-crossroads-shushening and

bagpipe-related myths. People who emigrated long, long ago told their kids about an Ireland frozen at the time of their leaving, and rose-coloured by distance and time. But we let them do it.

If you're after red-headed donkeys-and-carts, you just might be in for a nasty surprise. The donkeys are completely motorised now. But on the upside you'll be able to get a soya latte absolutely anywhere.

Ireland has changed. We'd all LOVE red hair, but dye is expensive and, believe us, it's practically impossible to keep a donkey in an upstairs flat in town – especially a motorised one.

Because we keep the changes quiet when it suits us, we probably have no right to give out when tourists hold up our ambulances. They probably think we drag our injured twice around fairy trees, but in fairness we're the ones who told them that. (Actually, you get treated quicker at the fairy tree, to be honest.)

So, tourists, we forgive you. But a little advice: stay up on that pavement. Those are real cars. We'd like you to make it home safely, to be sure, to be sure.

Moan factor: Diddly aye/Toora loora.

★

Tourism

★ The irrational fear of tourists and irrational fear of the lack of them ★

Despite all our moaning about tourists, we still desperately want them to come. Watch what happens if your town is left off a tourism map. *WAR*.

Periodically, the Tourist Board will launch some makey-uppy Way or Trail, invented to get tourists to a particular part of Ireland. Something like The Winsome West or Look, Here's Dublin! or Kilkenny Knitting: Unravelled or what-have-you. The knitter dollar isn't talked about enough.

Tourists spend a lot of time gazing patiently at what is essentially themed mud. They're taken to bare fields where once battles were fought, but where now there are only startled cows. They're quite nice about it, considering. (The tourists, that is. And the cows, to be fair.)

If your field or business – or, worse, your whole town – isn't highlighted on some little cartoon map that'll soon go into every hotel and airport, showing the way to the Way, go on the radio immediately and cry. You are being left behind. Not just geographically, but off the gravy train. No one likes missing the gravy train.

Never mind that your town already has plenty of visitors, a freshly rebranded muddy field and is directly accessible by rail: financial FOMO is enough to make any local tourism committee official burst, live on air.

They'll be on that feckin' map next year, though. We promise you that.

Moan factor: Where?/10

Máiréad writes to the local Tourist Board rep about having been narrowly map-missed by a Trail:

Dear Tony
Hope this finds you as it leaves me, well.

I've just received a copy of the lovely new map of the Timewarp Trail, which, as you know, was partly my idea. I clearly stated at our Let's Get On The 'Way' Bandwagon meeting that we should do something historical. I've never been a fan of Modern Ireland and I don't think it's something we should be showing to tourists either.

So imagine my surprise when I saw the map (which is lovely, did I mention that?) and noticed that the well near my house was not noted on it. I distinctly remember telling the committee about the well and how, while no miracles have occurred there and no wishes have come true, you couldn't say they wouldn't sometime.

Also, even though it was only dug in the seventies,

it's a nice stone well and the kind of thing tourists love to sit on and take selfies. I remember the committee being particularly 'fired up', I think the term is, about this. 'Selfies' and the like mean we can appeal to the younger tourist while still focusing firmly on the past.

As you know, my son Brian has a tea shop near the well, and he is very upset that he will not be getting well traffic now. A lot of people will be coming to the town on the Timewarp Trail and there's a good chance that his tea shop, Tea Shoppe, will be overlooked in favour of the other tea shop, teashop, which is on the trail. I notice your own wall is included, Tony, and it's just a wall. This is prejudice in the extreme.

I am nothing if not all about things that are good for the town and I think the Timewarp Trail is a fantastic idea. I should. I helped come up with it. Even if some people think there's a Rocky Horror tie-in, which there isn't. As you say, Tony, 'so long as they bring their fishnets to the town and do business'. I just wish Brian and I could have had a taste of it. The business, that is, not the fishnets.

Yours, in disappointment,
Máiréad

Television

★ Hitting the box a box ★

Before the internet, television shaped our view of the world. It was one of our only windows out.

Back when the majority of the country only had one station – RTÉ (just the one) – you'd have been forgiven for thinking the world itself was black and white, shushened, and peopled with politicians who'd seen action during the Rising. And that was just the children's programming.

American and British programmes showed us how people in other countries lived – IN COLOUR! – and also that there are different ways to spell 'colour'. It was very exciting altogether and many of us started speaking with an accent and calling our parents 'Ma' and 'Pa', even though we'd never even crossed our own county bounds. When the nation kind of *was* in black and white, riddled with unemployment, emigration and fear, colourdey shows from overseas were almost as good as a holiday. Nobody took foreign holidays then. You perched a caravan on a cliff in Connemara and hoped for the best.

So, now that we have satellite dishes and online streaming and have basically lost the televisual run of ourselves, what's there to moan about? Loads (duh):

* We moan about the shows' presenters: they're 'too dry', 'too flippant', or 'not "current affairsy" enough', or have 'no people skills'. Or they're 'too glam' or 'don't make an effort'. They can't win. It's great.

* Programming: there's either too much home-grown crap, or too much imported crap. Which is it, Ireland?

* We compare our domestic shows with those of bigger, more populated countries even though we just don't generate enough ad revenue: our budgets can't compete. It's a fecking miracle that we make anything even halfway decent when the sets are made of cereal packets and lit by Anglepoise lamps.

* We moan about how our national broadcaster is funded by ad revenue AND taxpayer money. Well, see above. Even with added licence fee and much moaning, it's still cereal packets for sets.

* We give out that there's too much 'youth' programming. That's true. There is. Especially when 'youth' programming is used as an excuse to make things even more cheaply than normal, the budget blown on neon clothes and Day-glo

paint. But a Day-glo-painted cereal packet is still a cereal packet.

* Hidden-camera shows replace comedy writing teams. Maybe write something sometime? Ah, we see. They're cheaper. Of course.

* We give out about why – in a country only stuffed with writers – Ireland can't produce something like *Breaking Bad*? If Walter White only had a cereal-packet set, he might never have made it out of the chemistry lab because it'd have caught fire. Now you know.

* Half of us moan about on-air bonging. The other half moans that there isn't nearly enough bonging on the airwaves and would happily pay for more.

* We give out that our actors can't act. They can. But you just try doing what they do with only a cereal packet for company.

At least we'll always have *The Late Late Show*. Always. For ever. Even after we are dead.

Moan factor: RTÉ1/10

Tea

★ There can be only one ★

We all know that Ireland is obsessed with tea and that tea is a magical elixir that makes everything alright. Many of us may have moved over to coffee more recently, but the cultural connection is still there.

But you should be aware that there are two kinds of tea:

The kind you drank growing up	All other kinds of tea
'Tea'	'Not tea' 'The other stuff' 'That shite' 'No'

For politeness' sake, this is often internalised, but it has been known to wreck relationships. Pair it with a slice of Battenberg and you're really living on the edge.

Moan factor: 10/10

★

U is for . . .

Unemployment

★ Giving out about this is a lifetime occupation ★

This is a serious issue that's been hanging over our heads for too long and one of the few things Irish people are perfectly justified in giving out about.

It's also like a longer form of one of our handy conversation-stoppers. The opposite of 'JOBS'– just say, 'Oh, yeah, well, *unemployment*', and the green-shoots merchants will shut up right quick.

Students have only ever really had one topic to prepare for oral exams: good old unemployment. So prep it and prep it hard, and then book a flight to Brussels to get yourself a job with that French degree.

The quest for work is what led to the scattering of the massive Irish diaspora and what continues to suck our kids over to Australia or wherever the current place is where the streets are paved with regular payslips and the promise of a pension.

So, go on: give out yards about unemployment. It really does seem to be part of the permanent fabric of the country now. It's never going to be properly addressed so we might as well get it out of our systems verbally.

Moan factor: 10/10

Scamall blogs on dropping out of the workforce years ago:

The last time I had a 'proper' job was in the mid-nineties. It was then I realised that I'm not the kind of person who can be a nine-to-five kind of person. My light was being hidden under a bushel of admin and drudgery. I have so much more to offer the world through my art and activism. Words are great and they have to be spoken, but we know a picture paints a thousand of them. Enda Kenny's not listening? Well, he can't unsee his own face, rendered in oils, with some really terrible eyebrows, now, can he? Artivism (art for activism) is undeniable.

Sometimes, I work two jobs – I'll leave a Dáil protest on Kildare Street and be up at the railings on Stephen's Green minutes later, selling my Kennys. No rest for the wicked.

MADE-UP FACT:

Bushels of Admin were a seventies Dublin band who came up with U2 but never made it. They were bitter for a while but then they started an office-supplies company under the same name and never looked back.

Underage . . . anything

★ Upping the ante ★

We're on our second U and nearly at the end of the alphabet. You're an expert at giving out at this stage and probably ready to take it to the next level.

If you want to give your moan a little extra edge, to elevate it from workaday gripe to pressing issue, just toss in the word 'underage'. Oh, the outrage you'll see then.

Adding 'underage' takes something that could, under other circumstances, be quite a fun Friday night (drinking, sex, truancy, gambling, sunbed use) and makes it ripe for really cross giving-out-about.

Make your complaint 'underage' and soon the *Livewhine* phones will be hopping. You see, we *do* care about our young people, whenever it comes to stopping them doing something.

Make sure not to offer any solutions, though: all you're after is a deeper, richer moan. A man-in-a-coffee-ad purr of a moan. Imagine that. Yep: creepy. But definitely give-out worthy.

If you can somehow steer the topic to Underage Unemployment, YOU WIN AT GIVING OUT. Not sure how Underage Unemployment would work, because underage kids are supposed to be unemployed so it wouldn't be a problem, but sure bring it up anyway. Máiréad would. Everyone will panic and the country's radios will melt. You won't need to turn the telly on for weeks and think of all the episodes of the Angelus you'll have backed up by then.

MADE UP FACT:

The Minister for Health is sending underage spies around to tanning salons to see if owners are letting under-eighteens use sunbeds*. Older people are faking their birth certs in order to volunteer in the hopes of a free tan. .

Moan factor: Off the scale.

U2

★ Begrudgery ★

The only giving-out topic as enduring as *Unemployment*. Ireland is divided when it comes to U2.

Our most successful export since red hair and cereals we've never heard of, they were our first world-famous rock band. It wasn't that there weren't great bands – there were tons of great bands – but they never made it outside Ireland. You might see them on *Top of the Pops* once or twice. But no one came close to the machine of fame and world domination that U2 were to become.

---

* This first bit is not made up.

When Bono pioneered the whole leaning-your-leg-on-a-monitor thing at Live Aid (getting some lunges in during the gig, before gyms were even popular), the world went crazy for the band from Dublin. Prior to that their TV appearances had been on shows like *Youngline*; shows with cereal-packet sets where they'd follow a topical discussion on – you guessed it – unemployment, or an item about Rice Krispie buns. Once the buns were made, stage hands saved the Rice Krispies packets for next week's set.

They were universally loved then. But once the world took notice of them, we could feel our giving-out muscles twitch. That was when the begrudgery really kicked in.

Here, we look at reasons we find for and against giving out about U2.

★

Reasons to give out about U2	In defence of U2
✳ Live Aid lunged them onto the global stage and they took to it like ducks to water. Famous, wealthy ducks. They seemed comfortable with fame, which Irish people aren't supposed to be, in case we think they think they're great.	✳ We're jealous. Of course we are. Jealous of the millions of euro and the monitor-toned thighs.
✳ They even looked cool in sunglasses – something none of the rest of us has managed before or since. Mad jealous, we were.	✳ We'd have better long-term eye health if we followed their example.

✳ What is that accent?	✳ Who cares how you say it, when what you're saying is that Ireland has the right to dream. Some day, if we worked really hard, we too could be their roadies and go on tour with them and lift their gear. Once we'd finished being a lift operator for Harrison Ford, of course.
✳ Something about tax (or whatever the story is there).	✳ They seem to employ at least a quarter of the population as roadies or fancy on-tour masseurs and the like. Lift operators too, probably. You can't argue with JOBS.

* There are two camps of U2 discovery according to the fervent U2 fans who knew the lads back in the Dandelion Market days: 1. the fervent U2 fans who knew the lads back in the Dandelion Market days; 2. anyone who discovered the band after Live Aid. They are 'too new'. They 'don't have history'. That's right. Twenty-five years of history – a quarter of a century – is not enough. Unless 'you were there' you're not allowed to like U2. You're 'too new'.

* Unless you're one of the fervent U2 fans who knew the lads back in the Dandelion Market days, you've no right to defend U2. You weren't there.

A word of caution, though, U2 lads: like all Irish celebrities, half of us went to school with you. So while half of us are diehard fans, you can take it as read the other half is going, 'What's that feckin' eejit doing on TV?'

Tom in his cab:

'Bono can't get served in the centre of Dublin. That's a fact. Forget pints – sure he can't go out. Once, he waited a whole afternoon to have his shoes resoled. And because he didn't want to remind people about the taxes thing, whatever the story is there, he didn't complain, even though the heel place did all the other jobs first: stilettos, hiking boots, pet tags, you name it. It's a disgrace and a national tragedy. I mean he may be an eejit, but aren't we all? And besides, JOBS.'

NB: pretty much everyone agrees that shoving an unasked-for album onto your iTunes is a little pushy. Back in the day, you'd never have broken into someone's house with a cassette and shoved it into their tape player. 'Larry would have been morto', someone who knew the lads back in the Dandelion Market days will say, shaking their head, supping a pint that Bono – tragically – will never be able to order.

Let's not fight about this. Let's just put on our big shades and hold our lighters in the air.

Moan factor: One/10

V is for . . .

Vagina Owners

★ What will we do about the women, at all? ★

And speaking of not giving a tuppenny shit about women
. . . Well, we weren't, but we might as well have been.

Having a vagina in Ireland isn't much fun. Owning one
makes life an awful lot trickier. A lot of people don't like
to talk about them – like, at all – but, as ever, somehow we
still find ways to give out about them.

You can't go around saying 'vagina' every time the
pesky owner of one does something pesky. Saying it
aloud is too shocking. Vaginas, as we all know, are
shameful and deeply suspect. So we have euphemisms
for them so exclusive that even other English speakers
won't know what we're on about. (NB: it's vaginas.) 'Gee'
(pronounced *ghee*) we'll say, and everyone thinks we're
into Indian cookery. We may also be into Indian cookery,
but we're actually referring to lady parts.

> Tom, on just about anything:
>
> 'I've a pain in the gee from it.'

Yes, even blokes can have a pain in their imaginary gee
– but only if the thing they're giving out about is so bad

it can only be compared to a pain in something utterly shameful.

There are a couple of things which, as a vagina owner, you should never buy in order to spare the blushes of everyone else and avoid being given out about in a very uncomfortable way:

1. Tampons: Until fairly recently, only the brave bought these. It was tantamount to admitting you were either a vagina owner yourself, or vagina-owner adjacent. You practically had to hold the pharmacist at gunpoint with a balaclava over your head in a bid to protect your own dignity and that of the pharmacist, who'd be forced to acknowledge the existence of the menstrual cycle. That acknowledgement involves thinking about vaginas and, somewhere beyond that, wombs. Unfertilised ones, which just isn't the way Ireland traditionally likes its wombs.

2. Vagina owners should never, ever, EVER buy condoms. Condoms imply that you intend using your vagina for pleasure. The pharmacist is duty-bound to produce a sawn-off shotgun from under the counter and dispatch you. At the trial, 'Exhibit A: Pleasure sheaths'. CASE CLOSED. She was a hussy. But, then, that's just the kind of thing vagina owners are always at.

MADE-UP FACT

In the past, when unmarried vaginas were stupid enough to let sperm get past them and into the womb, they were moved to free-range vagina farms where they were given lots of hay to eat and meadows to frolic in.

Not so made up, but just as outlandish, unmarried vaginas were actually sent to what are now known by the forgetful as 'Lovely Laundries'. There, they were protected from men and themselves by having their babies sold to America. Sure, how could a vagina look after a baby? Don't be ridiculous. Vaginas weren't 'real' mothers, so they were put to lovely work at what they were good at: making sure things were lovely and clean. Next time you have a stain to get out, ask a vagina! Thousands of nuns can't be wrong.

Nowadays, the Lovely Laundries are gone and there are free-range vaginas all over the place. Vaginas with notions. All non-vagina fans have left is the fact that vaginas still don't have a say over their own wombs. Vaginas allowing their shameful selves to get involved in crisis pregnancies must follow through no matter what, or feck off to England to get it sorted there so we don't have to think about it. It's all too tiring.

Vaginas are trouble. Vaginas are icky. Vaginas really

would give you a pain in the gee. No wonder the poor, poor politicians are over them.

Moan factor: Repeal the 8th/10

Ciarán talks to Jer about women:

'Women are so unreasonable. You know? Really needy and that. From what I've seen online they're just pains in the arse. It's all "feminist this" and "You're a creep" that. I'd LOVE to call myself a feminist but I never would because, then what? I'm not allowed slut-shame if a girl lets herself down online? How else is she going to learn?'

Vests (See Pneumonyeah!)

W is for . . .

Weather

★ Wet 'n' wild 'n' whiny ★

If *Potholes* are a go-to, a giving-out home, weather is our default giving-out setting. If you switch an Irish person off and back on again, when we reboot, we'll be giving out about this.

We'll go ahead and lump weather together with another W, because the perception is that it's permanently winter here. It is not permanently winter. It's just *mostly* like that. No wonder we need to get it off our vest-clad chests. (See *Pneumonyeah!*)

The truth is that if the weather itself could really make us sick, we'd all be long dead. Rather, it's made us hardy and proud of it. Every one of us has 'summer' family beach or barbecue pictures in which the outstanding feature is pairs of bright-blue legs.

MADE-UP FACT

Irish 'summer' pictures were the inspiration for the Na'vi in *Avatar*.

Wind is another brilliant weather moan. We get only loads of it, and it's incredibly destructive. There's so much to give out about with wind:

* It knocks down gable walls.

* It means no Irish person can have a hairdo.

* Kiting is out of the question, unless you fancy ending up in Wales. (Actually, that sounds quite nice.)

* It sweeps umbrellas and people off cliffs, creating drama in books like *Peig*.

* It spawns lazy programmes like *Worst Wind Warnings of the West*, with fly-on-the-wet-wall footage of people rowing around the sitting room on a raft that used to be their couch.

We're obsessed with the weather and there's plenty of it to give out about. No wonder our cheeky TV weather people are insta-celebs. Just add water. And wind.

Moan factor: Constant low hum with an upsurge in the winter months, which are year-round/10

Women (See Vagina Owners and Zygotes)

★ These sections sum up the giving out about us, really. But anyway . . . ★

Moan factor: Loud

X is for . . .

★ Yes, we're cheating on the X words, but you're going to have to let it pass. There are very few X words to give out about in Irish society. Not really. There isn't even an X in the

Irish language, so we obviously don't have a lot of time for it. X-rays? They're actually pretty great. Nothing to give out about there, bar a bit of radiation. Xylophone? Who hates xylophones? Serial killers, maybe, but only them. To make up for our lack of X beefs, we've decided to have guest appearances from topics featuring big Xs in their midst ★

SeXual Healing

★ When I think about you I don't touch myself ★

We could give out about this for ever. Oh! It's our favourite. It was certainly the worst, according to Dev and ABJCMcQ.

Never before has the supposed lack of something so defined a nation. We complained for decades about not being able to have it for fun, but we somehow still had it all the time and made millions of babies – and now others complain that there's just too much of it everywhere. The fun kind! Down with sexy fun!

The truth is that we really are mad-sexy little fellas altogether, and gods alone know who we'd have been if we'd been allowed to keep our ancient pagan sex positivity and sexy festivals. The reason we had such big families pre-contraception is that – even though we knew we'd been shushened and told not to have it – we just couldn't stop having sex. The weather was awful and there was no telly: what else were we supposed to do?

A lot of the people who give out about sex on the radio in a moany way (no, not that kind of moaning – although it does seem to give them a lot of pleasure) are those who seem obsessed with the sex lives of others. Other than that, these days you're as likely to hear a 'sexpert' on our airwaves as on those of any other country.

Most of us feel a lot more comfortable talking about sex and gender issues in general because recently we've been given the space to rediscover our inner pagan. It was only when The Shushening shushed us up that we were unhappy. Now we're allowed to love sex again, and allow for the fact that different people like to do it in different ways. And that's great! But not to the ladies and gentlemen of Máiréad's society, the Order of the Genitals (OOG).

> She doesn't like you to bring it up but, of course, Máiréad is head, neck and heels of the OOG. And sex is her favourite thing to love to hate writing to the papers about:
>
> *Dear Sir*
> *It has come to my attention that, in the 'modern' Ireland of ours, everyone is having sex all the time. And not the good kind – the kind that had in shame in the dark with the sole intention of having a baby at the end of it – the*

bad kind: the kind had for fun by people I don't know and have no intention of meeting. This doesn't stop me obsessing about their genitals and where they're putting those genitals, though. Oh, no. It is my duty to tell everyone why they should be thinking about other people's genitals and, in fact, be terrified of them.

Sodomy is coming into Ireland like a big truck, driving around and forcing people to get into the back of it. And when you get on the sodomy truck, you can't get off. There are no brakes and it's perched on the top of a hill to Hell. And that's where you're going if you have sodomy or support sodomy or even if you don't know what it is but aren't so terrified of the whole idea of it that you fall asleep screaming in case a gay comes into your bedroom and makes you do it, despite your thick protective layers of nightgown and prayer. I was only saying this to my husband, whom I see as far more than a penis on legs, even though that is what we at OOG reduce everyone else to: people are essentially genitals, but dangerous genitals, because they're genitals with ideas.

The lot that call themselves 'inclusive' are killed saying that non-man-woman sex can be an expression of love and commitment. But it can't, because I can't get my head around that. I even hesitate to use the word 'head' in case someone misunderstands and uses this against me on Twitter, saying that I'm pro talking about genitals in an open forum. I am not. They should be kept behind closed doors, and if you're using them in any way like I imagine you are if you're a same-sex couple, then those doors should be those of a prison. Now, I never said that, so please don't remind me of it.

There is a reason that homosexual acts were illegal: it is because they're way too sexy for most of us to handle and could easily warp a young mind into thinking that sex should be fun. It should not. Sex should be dutifully done by your husband to you and if you don't have a husband, you should make sure your hands are always in oven gloves to keep you from temptation. I still keep mine by the bed whenever my husband is away.

It's not just the homosexuals, though: they're just an obvious target. There are loads of other names you're supposed to remember now. It's all 'bi' this and 'trans' that. I can't keep all that in my head. So called 'straights' are probably up to all sorts in privacy too, and I swear that I will make it my life's work to make sure that all sex is preceded by a decade of the rosary and a camera feed from the bed (it must be done in a bed) direct to the parochial house, where several prominent parishioners can view the sex being had and make sure it's not deviant in any way. I spoke to the bishop after last week's Confirmation and he said he'd be up for it. So that's that sorted.

Please, please, make sure you think about other people's terrifying genitals. The way Ireland is going, I feel like we at the OOG are the only ones still focused on this. Nobody else seems bothered but I'm sure I've caught something just thinking about it.

Better terror and oven gloves than driving us all to Hell on a sodomy truck; a truck, I fear, that has no brakes.

Mise, le meas

Máiréad O'B of the OOG

Poor old Máiréad, We're afraid the only orgasm she has is when she finishes typing one of these breathless letters. But that's entirely her own business.

Moan factor: 6/10

TaXis

★ I'll take you home again, Kathleen, if you know where you're going and you have the exact fare ★

A lovely treat when you're tired after a heavy supermarket shop, or a safe way to get home after a night on the town, right?

Wrong.

We can even give out about this. You should know that by now – we're already on X.

Before the Celtic Tiger mauled us with his big, stripy paws, it was almost impossible to get a cab. The cost of a taxi plate was so prohibitive that you really had to want to drive people around pretty badly. Only the most dedicated natural-born cabbies or the off spring of rich merchants achieved it, so there were only about fifteen taxis in the land. This meant that at two a.m. on a Saturday morning, something like seventy thousand people (that's what it felt like, anyway) all tried to squeeze into the same cabs, while the queues snaked for miles. In fact, you'd probably have got home more quickly if you'd crowd-surfed, being handed down the line, over people's heads. Good way to meet people, too.

When they made the plates more affordable, suddenly there were loads more taxis on the streets and we didn't know ourselves. We were able to get home before five a.m.! It was a miracle. Many suffered retina damage from the glare of the lights of available cabs – it was so bright, it was sort of what we imagined living somewhere sunny must be like.

MADE-UP FACT

Taxis were so plentiful, people would take one from the bus stop to their door, then try to convince the driver to drive them up the stairs.

We love a good nose into other people's business, and taxi drivers get all the good goss. They are like shamans, or modern-day druids – dispensing unasked-for wisdom and cursing people they don't like. They are also experts at choosing the ambient sounds for every mood: not that they choose the *right* background noise but, somehow, they can enhance however you're feeling with just a flip of the dial. If you're feeling chilled, they'll find something mellow. If you're already wound tight and don't want to talk, how, oh, how do they know to wind you up even tighter with racist talk radio? So soothing. It's a skill.

There's been some controversy lately over who will get into whose cabs, based on the colour of the skin of the driver. Excuses are made: non-native Irish drivers 'just don't know the place like the Irish fellas, that's all I'm sayin''. But really we do know what they're saying. You always know what a taxi driver is saying, because – if they're like Tom – they'll just say it.

A few random real-life nuggets from taxi drivers encountered recently:

1. 'The courtesy's come back onto the roads since austerity. People lost the run of themselves when they had money. Now, they're driving nicer.'

2. 'Women! No offence. You see them in the morning, driving with the windows all fogged

up. They can't see out. Dropping the kids to school. Blind. Always women. It's what has the roads the way they are at rush-hour, the women in the fogged-up cars. No offence.'

3. 'You only have fifty euro? What do you think I am, a bank? I never even kicked you in the eye!'

4. *On hearing that a parent passed away that morning:* 'You know what you need, love? Elvis. Elvis makes everything alright.' *Puts on Elvis. Drives without a word.*

5. *On 22 May, Referendum Day:* 'I dunno. It's 2015. I think we're all equal. But I did hear a lot of them immigrants were voting No.'

6. *Later that same night, different cab:* 'I heard, this gay marriage, you'll be able to get a divorce after a day.' *For balance.*

7. 'Where's that again? Never heard of it. I don't believe it exists. I'll take you where I think you should live.'*

As you can see, cabbies are so wise it seems almost churlish to give out about them. Also, a cab is a microcosm of the nation's giving out distilled, over a ten-minute journey, into its purest form. That's just good science.

---

* This one may not be fully true, but it's very close.

A journalist from the evening paper follows Tom for 'A Night in the Life of a Cabbie'. Tom is only too happy to chat:

'I start work about seven o'clock. In the evening, like. I don't like to get people straight after work, I prefer to get them when they've a few jars on them and they've chilled out a bit. No pukin', though. I know where they live, I'll come after them!

'I've had them all in my cab: Ryan Tubridy, Dana, yer man who does the houses on the telly, that chef, Michelle Heaton off of Liberty X, Angela Lansbury and Twink. Not one of them had to clean out the cab, I can tell you. Class acts, the lot of them. I'd a ghost in the cab once. You don't have to believe me, but I did. Dame Street. Yeah.

'You see it all in this job. If you want to know where the best falafel in a town is, ask your driver. We'd go out of our way for it and the Middle Eastern lads tells us where they're at. Rolls are ancient history.

'Yeah, way more Middle Eastern lads on the job now. Way more. African fellas too. But I still can't look at women driving cabs. I'm not a sexist, but I do think men are better drivers, now. No shame in it. Women are great talkers but they're hardly great parkers, are they? The female brain – it's different. Strengths and weaknesses, swings, roundabouts.

'I think people prefer a male driver, cos the strong silent type makes them feel safer.'

Silent, Tom? Chance would be a fine thing.
Moan factor: 4/10

TaXes

★ Turning people upside down and shaking the cents out of them ★

We all hate taxes – especially U2, or whatever the story is there. But we know we have to pay them to make the country work. And our government likes to raise the bar for creatively getting the money out of people. It's enough to make our blood boil – just like the water we can't afford.

For instance, there was the Universal Social Charge, presumably so-called because it went . . . somewhere . . . in the . . . universe. You might as well call it the 'Just Cos tax'.

In terms of good giving out, simply say the phrase 'taxpayers' money' or 'my hard-earned cash' repeatedly, when you wonder aloud why the potholes haven't been fixed yet. No one will disagree; in fact, they might just explode in angry agreement.

Sadly, the energy spent moaning about these things means we forget to actually, practically, press for important things, like childcare and housing, in exchange for the taxes. If we thought we were getting them, we might even look at paying more.

That said, we know we won't get them because 'they' are all the same, just like the other shower.

But you know us! Even if some day we were to get value for our taxes, we wouldn't let that get in the way of a good giving out.

Moan factor: 20 to 40%/10

Y is for . . .

Youth

★ . . . is wasted, etc. ★

We talk a lot about our young people. We might as well, because we don't do much for them.

We give out non-stop about how there's nothing for them here, but the hand-wringing rings a bit hollow as nothing changes to make them stay.

MADE-UP FACT

We actually secretly want them to go so we've somewhere to stay in Sydney.

It's hard to be young in Ireland. Not only do you have all the modern-day stresses – exam worries, cyber-bullying, being great for cheap labour, the fact that you'll have to admit you met your partner on Tinder – but the truth is that no one in Ireland is ever truly young.

It's the constant giving out. Babies in the womb in other countries get Mozart played to them; here, it's talk radio on tap, the sweet-sweet music of moaning from the get-go. What chance do we have? We arrive out of the birth canal wailing like aul' fellas and keep it up for another eight decades or so.

We still expect The Shushening to leap out and stop us doing something, so our brows are perma-furrowed, our hair pre-greyed. Youth is supposed to be a carefree time, but we Irish don't have carefree in our genes. Craic, yes – and our young people have plenty of that. But the burden of history alone is enough to age you on the spot.

Pity the poor kids who grew up in Celtic Tiger times. They're the ones looking bewildered at the airport as they're shoved onto the plane by even more bewildered-looking parents, who naively thought we'd be able to give them prospects – maybe even prosperity – here at home.

But we completely forgot to give them tools. We didn't teach them the good survival stuff we'd learned pre-old Stripy Paws:

What we should have taught kids	What we actually taught them
✳ How to browse second-hand shops, without irony.	✳ €400 was what shoes cost.
✳ Mandarin.	✳ English was the only language they would ever need.
✳ How to get six dinners out of a can of baked beans and a potato.	✳ That they didn't need to study maths – sure, wasn't that what accountants were for?
✳ That dentists are a luxury item.	✳ That teeth-whitening was the right of every citizen.

➡

* That they don't really need to be paid.

* If an 'employer' offers you 'experience' or 'exposure' in lieu of payment, and they're being paid, say you'll pass, because you'll get both quicker by waiting till you're ninety, or streaking down Grafton Street. Exposure, your arse.

No wonder young people give out: that early taste of the Tiger made reality way harder for them.

And when we did have money, did we invest it in education or resources for kids in less advantaged areas? No, we didn't.

Tigers aren't the scary ones. We are.

Moan factor: 9/10

Seán talks to Jer about his and Betty's decision not to have kids:

'It wasn't that we couldn't, Jer. We just didn't want to. Sure, look at the state of the place, Jer. I'm not sure it's right. The way things are the last while, we'd only be rearing them for export, and that's tough enough with a favourite cow. I don't know how you'd say goodbye to your child.'

Yer Man

★ Giving out about the man on the street, or at your elbow ★

We are fiercely loyal.

Gotcha!

We would never let loyalty or anything else get in the way of a good bitching session. This section is about giving out about other people.

'Yer man' (or 'yer woman') is how the Irish refer to someone when they either don't know, or don't want to say, their name. It's particularly useful when you want to moan or complain about someone within earshot. If you play this risky game right, they will never know you were giving out about them. In the hands of a master, people have even been known to join in on a bitching session about themselves.

We are a very welcoming people, say all the ads and postcards. But we've seen enough in this book to know that too much of that touchy-feely-welcomey stuff makes us uncomfortable. We only really put up with people till they move out of earshot and we get the opportunity to say how rubbish they are. In a nice friendly way. Round the corner.

'Yer man' enables us to do so even if they're taking their time about shifting.

If you'd prefer not to be given out about, good luck! You will be.

Here are reasons why Yer Man or Yer Woman – a perfectly nice man or woman to begin with – might become 'an awful bollix altogether' and get given out about.

'Yer man is an awful bollix altogether' because:

* He never gets his round in.

* He gets his round in, but not quickly enough for your liking.

* He always gets his round in, throwing his money around making everyone else look stingy.

* He thinks he's great. Did you see him wearing the sunglasses, there?

* He's seeing a grand lad's wife behind his back.

* He sent in his Irish Water form first go, with his real name on it.

* He's a politician.

* He's a pro-choice feminist.

* He's a pro-life misogynist.

* He's a bit of both of the above.

* He's very fit and therefore 'up himself'.

* He has the wrong kind of accent.

* He's a name-dropper who pretends to know all kinds of powerful or famous people. Like yer woman and yer man – you do know them. (Ah, you do.)

* He really does know all kinds of powerful or famous people, like yer woman and yer man, but he won't introduce you to yer man who could give you a dig-out.

If you're unlucky enough to find yourself at the receiving end of a direct 'Yer man', 'Yer woman' or 'Yer wan' (accompanied by a confirming flick of the head in your direction), the best thing is to laugh.

Pretend you just don't care. You *are* a bollix and you're cool with that. Owning it is the only way out.

Moan factor: 2/10 (We secretly enjoy being talked about)

Z is for . . .

Let Zygotes be Zygotes

★ Womb with a view? ★

And so we come almost full circle. Way back in A we met the unsayable *Aborshhh* . . . Now in Z, we meet another word you shouldn't really say. Even if you're a man. But you'll probably only really need this word if you're a stupid vagina owner and now you're pregnant and want to discuss your options.

From the second of conception in Ireland, BAM!, what's in the womb is 'a child'. Even if the sperm and egg have barely been on a date yet and don't even know each other's last names. 'A child', in the womb, there, installing a swing-set and applying for schools. The stupid vagina owner is an insta-mother now, just how we like our women here. Now she has a purpose, unlike when she was just a stupid vagina owner. Now she's fulfilling the right role and can probably spontaneously cook better and everything.

Dev and ABJCMcQ would be delighted that such comely maidens are still living out their fantasies to this day, whether we like it or not.

Use terms like 'zygote' or 'foetus' (or even 'autonomy' or 'choice'), and you're no longer toeing the party line.

You're drawing attention to the fact that there actually isn't 'a child' – not yet. But why would you draw attention to that? You're about to be a mother, like it or not, and get better at cooking! Your husband will love that (you have one, right? You're pregnant), and your child will be only delighted with the improved cakes. Why not just accept that it's a child from the get-go and buy that tiny collapsible swing-set?

Here's why: you're heartless. You hate kids, especially babies, and you don't want them to have swings. You're a kind of selfish half-woman with no intention of fulfilling the potential someone else has set out for you, like a lovely olden-days dress you should put on you. It's much more womanly. You aren't the kind of woman people *really* like: meek, smiling, bent on self-sacrifice and saying, 'Yes!' all the time, when asked for more tea.

'You're not lovely, like we like. You don't wear flowery dresses. You're awful, like we don't like. And you hate babies.'

So you're better off pretending words like 'zygote' don't exist, because they'll only reveal your selfish plans to destroy civilisation. Awful woman.

In fact, we don't even need the 'awful'; just 'woman'. By which, of course, we mean Stupid Vagina Owner.

Moan factor: 0/10 (This word is all but banned)

The last word on this has to go to Máiréad —
who else? — in a national paper:

A chara

*I'm sick of reading articles in your paper by 'progressive',
'pro-choice' women. This is somehow suggesting that
people like me hate to choose or let others choose. This
is absolutely not the case. Just this morning I left my
husband two shower-gel options. Yes, I left one slightly
ahead of the other, but only because I know he really
likes mint. He'd be lost without me.*

*You know what else would be lost without people
like me? This country. If everyone could choose what
they thought was best there'd be utter chaos. You
wouldn't let a child have all the sweets, would you?
Well, discipline is necessary for adults, too. The bad
kind of adult, anyway. Unmarried women. It's even
hard for me to type that.*

*Everyone should have the right to choose certain
things, according to a certain set of rules. Individuals
have been getting their way too much lately and we
have to halt that before we drive this country off a cliff.
First the sodomy truck and now this.*

*If a woman goes to order a sandwich, wouldn't it
be nice if there were an authority figure there in the
sandwich shop to kindly suggest she be forced to eat*

a salad instead? Women are so busy now with all the independence and everything that we don't have time to think clearly. We're tired. We need someone to tell us what decisions to make. I'm happy to do it.

When I say to a woman that 'life's full of suffering', I'm being as kind as I can. I noted she was suffering, didn't I? I'm not saying a woman is only a vessel: I'm saying she's a vessel among other things. Please don't put words in my mouth. I don't like having anything in my mouth against my will.

A discredited online study found that women who go to England to get aborshhh . . . and break the law here will get a taste for the law-breaking and all turn to lives of crime within five years. Is it really so bad to suggest putting them straight into jail as soon as they're sexually active, for their own good?

We tried something like that before. It could work again.

Yours BY CHOICE
Máiréad, OOG

And, with that, we're finished our giving-out alphabet.

If you don't live here, now you can blend in like a native, from A to Z.

If you do live here, here's something for us to think

about: would it really be so bad if we just agreed for a bit? Or left something unsaid? Do we have to give out yards about everything?

To be honest, we probably do. Imagine how isolated we'd become if we weren't unified by bitching on the radio or in the papers or online? The country would crumble.

And, actually, if you were to believe the giving out, it already has.

So let's meet for a pint and give out yards.

DVD Extras

We know DVDs don't really exist anymore, but while you're giving out about that, here are your extra scenes.

------------------------------------✂------------------------------------

To cut out and keep in your wallet or close to your heart:

The Ten Commandments of Giving Out Yards

1. Thou art lord of this giving out. They shalt not take other callers before thee.

2. Thou canst not take thyself too seriously, ever.

3. Remember, Sunday is still a great day for giving out. Rest ye not.

4. Honour thine iMOM and thine iMOM-in-law,

thy kin and all the rest of the relatives, but only if they're within earshot. Otherwise, give out about them, too.

5. Thou shalt not kill or rape or other bad stuff and go to prison if you know the judge or are a 'grand lad'.

6. Thou shalt not commit adultery and take part in more than one call-in if you've agreed to talk to Jer.

7. Thou shalt not steal someone else's giving-out thunder, unless you interject quickly with 'Let me finish' often enough.

8. Thou shalt not bear false witness. Not really! Bear it and bear it hard so long as it helps to beef up your argument.

9. Thou shalt not covet thy neighbour's debating skill. Do not listen to their point of view lest ye be swayed.

10. Thou art right, and thou willst always be right. Stick to thy guns and do not be deterred by 'facts' or other obstacles.

It is thy divine right to moan. Go ye, be fruitful, multiply your worries and woes, yet attempt ye not to solve them.

In other words, give ye out yards.

Amen.

------------------------------------>✂-----------------------------------

An Interview with Jer

I am late. I didn't mean to be but the traffic in this town
... well ... I console myself that he'd know more about
that than most. He certainly gets an earful of traffic every
day.

I swirl frantically up the staircase (it's swirly) and
fling myself into the upstairs bar where I'm supposed
to be meeting one of Ireland's most familiar voices, but
most elusive personalities. I'm late to talk to Jer – yes,
the Jer – and I'm mortified.

I dive into the bar and he's already there, composed,
giving out autographs to a couple of lady shoppers.
He has already ordered tea. For both of us. What a
gentleman. The ladies depart, elated, and I huff and puff
my apologies, peeling off cycling gear as I do. 'You came
on the bike, did you?' says Jer. Nothing escapes this
man. With a flourish, he pours me tea.

As I compose myself, his phone goes off. The ringtone?
'O Donnell Abú'. Of course it is. As he indicates that
he must take this, the tone in that familiar voice is
somehow both apologetic and unrepentant at once, so
for a moment, I don't move. I daren't. Jer notices my

unease, and – phone tucked beneath his chin – offers me one of the cookies arranged on an ornate plate on a table in front of us. Chocolate chip. And here I'd thought he'd be scones all the way.

But such powerful men are always complex.

A mere few minutes of pacing later and the call comes to an end. 'I don't like to keep people waiting, but business is business, you know?'

I did know. And Jer's business is chat. Or more specifically, complaint. There are those who say that without Jer, the country would have gone to the dogs altogether years ago, so I can't believe this legend has agreed to give me an exclusive interview. Or that I'd kept him waiting in the first place, yet not a grumble out of him. Perhaps he gets enough of that sort of moany thing at work. Perhaps he has no time for giving out in his downtime.

He breathlessly settles in to the armchair opposite mine, tucking his long, girlish legs up under him and nibbling around the edges of one of the cookies, leaving practically no teeth marks at all. When he speaks, it sounds like that iconic voice is coming through an old gramophone horn, direct from the past. Yet it is clear and present. He's dressed comfily.

'Is that an Aran onesie?' I ask. He laughs (but not for long). Yes, not a lot of people know that he knits. That's not all a lot of people don't know. I clear my throat, and shoot at him. Questions, that is.

Q. Please don't take this the wrong way, but I can't find anything about you online.

A. Ah yes. I work very hard to maintain my privacy. I've a small but permanent team to take down my Wikipedia page as soon as it goes up.

Q. Why so elusive?

A. Well, I'm here now, aren't I? He expertly repositions a pulled Aran yarn using a spoon handle.

Q. Yes. But you never really talk about yourself in interviews. I'm wondering if you'll give us anything juicy this time?

A. Laughter. You know, I have a full life. But people don't really want to know about it. If they did, they'd ask me whenever they called into the show, or wrote in to a paper. But they don't. They just want to let off some steam. I'm like a therapist they don't have to pay – at least, not directly! I have to be like an empty pint glass: the nation needs to pour its troubles into me, and let them settle. If there were already something in the glass, where would we be? Sure, the head would never be right.

Q. Do you think Irish people enjoy giving out?

A. That goes without saying.

Q. Ah, say it.

A. Irish people love giving out. It's good for them.

Q. Some people say that the outlet you give them – daytime airtime, night-time shock chat – means they

never have to take action. That in many ways, the
giving out is unhealthy: a self-perpetuating thing.

A. I think it's true that, after we've vented, we feel
like that's it. Done. We've had our say and now let
someone else get their dander up and actually wave a
fist. Doing it on air appeals to our sense of drama. And
it's symbolic. Séamas or Susan or whoever can go into
work the next day and be a watercooler hero. They
went on the radio or into a TV studio audience and
ranted on everyone else's behalf. Don't minimise that
experience either: I don't think it's overdramatic to
say the media – including social media – is a modern-
day battleground. Séamas and Susan and the rest of
them are warriors. In a very real sense it's every bit as
exhausting as hand to hand combat.

Q. Who do you wish would call in?

A. You mean like a fantasy guest?

Q. Yes.

A. I'd love to get Archbishop John Charles McQuaid
and Eamon de Valera into the studio. Set the record
straight, you know? Cookie? (He offers me the plate
again.) Hindsight's twenty/twenty, we all know that
now. They were different times and it's amazing how
literally people can take you once stuff gets written
down. But that bromance is still affecting this country
in so many ways. I'd love to know more, for the
country's sake. Did they call each other to decide on

outfits? Did they have sleepovers? Did they really believe that women are awful and all that, or does either of them regret The Shushening and feel a bit morto about it? Do they think we should grab Catholic conservatism by the balls – really go for it for once and for all – or move on and forge a new Ireland? I can tell you this much: the switch would be hopping. Those lads are a hot button.

Q. You're not on Twitter yourself?

A. The team is. I pop on the odd time, for a look. But people have enough access. They can't be in my ear twenty-four/seven. I'd lose it completely. You have to have a clear delineation: public vs private. Otherwise it's just blurred lines.

(He half smiles and hums a little 'Blurred Lines' to himself.)

Q. You like Robin Thicke?

A. Actually, I'm more of a Pharrell man, myself.

Q. I wouldn't have thought you'd have had time for modern music!

A. Modern? That was 2013, Grandma.

(At this point, one of his team – a young, scrubbed-looking fellow in a suit that's much too big for him – pops up unexpectedly from behind a nearby high-backed chair. I nearly drop my cookie with the fright. He nods curtly at me, and whispers in Jer's ear. He then taps his watch disapprovingly and vanishes behind the high-back again.)

A. I'm sorry, we'll have to wrap this up. Giving out gives out no days off!

(He laughs, presumably at saying 'giving out' twice in a row, but whatever it's about, I realise I'll have to get to the nub of things. The lad in the suit looked like he might take a bullet for Jer... or put one in me.)

Q. Why do you think the Irish are such great givers out?

A. We're a nation of contradictions. Always have been. We pair a beautiful ancient fighting spirit with low self-esteem. It leaves us stymied altogether. We're pulled in all directions: tradition – modernity. Misery – craic. Religion – sexy paganism. We're only finding out where all that has left us. It's good to talk. And that's what I'm here for. If I hadn't, it'd have been somebody else. In fact, it often is.

(With that, the young aide re-emerges and it's clear he means business. He needs to spirit Jer to his next appointment, wherever he is needed most: listening at the end of a phone; nodding in response to a long, beautifully written letter that will, in itself, be all the action the writer will take; resident, most certainly, in our hearts. Jer pays for the tea – he won't hear of anything less – and shakes my hand firmly and warmly. And in a flash of Aran onesie, he is gone.)

Acknowledgements

THANKS: THE OPPOSITE OF GIVING OUT YARDS

To Mum and Sara: if we can get through this year, eh? To Brendan and Andy. To Diarmuid O'Brien and Deirdre Sullivan. To John and Neil. To John Fox. Vincent and Hilary. Orlaith, Mick and Mily. Carrie and Ross. To Wendy, Stephen, Max and Bella. To Maria and Kieran. Katia and John. Abie and Adrianna. Michelle and Dermot. Jim, Eimear and family. Sinéad Gleeson and Anna Carey. Amy Herron and the Irish Writers Centre. Everyone at Blinder and Irish Pictorial Weekly. Everyone at Deadpan Pictures. Dublin Comedy Improv. Everyone at Petsitters Ireland. Julian Benson Management and Mandy Ward Artist Management. Voicebank. To everyone who voted

YES to equality in Ireland and gave some of us less to give out about, others loads more. To Barbara Scully, Caroline Grace Cassidy, Dave Rudden, Colm O'Gorman, Louise O'Neill, Róisín Ingle, Janet Ní Shuilleabháin, Paul Howard, Anthea McTeirnan, Jason Kennedy, Carol Hunt, Donal O'Keeffe, Sali Hughes, Kate Beaufoy, Marian Keyes and everyone else who gave me a good loving kick of inspiration whenever I was giving out, up, or in. To Ciara Considine, Joanna Smyth and all at Hachette for their kindness, understanding, patience and damn good steers throughout this process and never, ever making it feel like giving out. To my lovely Carl for giving me little to give out about, even though he has yards to give out about himself. And to Oscar.